More praise for *It Can't Rain All the Time*

"*It Can't Rain All the Time* is criticism, history, memoir,
and poetry: a work of art about a work of art."
— Matt Zoller Seitz, author of *The Wes Anderson Collection*

"Alisha Mughal writes beautifully, vulnerably, and
viscerally. *It Can't Rain All the Time* is a powerful reminder
that the most powerful art reminds us how to feel."
— Anne T. Donahue, author of *Nobody Cares*

"Meticulously researched and brilliantly presented, Mughal
unpacks *The Crow*'s raw beauty and aching grief — themes
that resonate at the core of both James O'Barr's graphic
novel and the iconic 1994 film adaptation. This is more than
analysis; it's a tribute to the emotional weight and artistic
legacy that *The Crow* continues to carry."
— Carleigh Baker, author of *Last Woman*

"This book is a sheer, dark gem that glints and pulses at the
very intersection of life and death. Alisha Mughal writes with
searing intelligence, exactitude, and soul about heartbreak
as a generative force and art as a site of resurrection.
Through the prismatic lens of a cult film and its dead star,
Mughal finds her own hard-won salvation. Daring, gory, and
radiant, *It Can't Rain All the Time* is ultimately that rarest of
offerings: an act of faith and
— Claudia Dey, auth

# the pop classics series

- **#1** *It Doesn't Suck. Showgirls*
- **#2** *Raise Some Shell. Teenage Mutant Ninja Turtles*
- **#3** *Wrapped in Plastic. Twin Peaks*
- **#4** *Elvis Is King. Costello's My Aim Is True*
- **#5** *National Treasure. Nicolas Cage*
- **#6** *In My Humble Opinion. My So-Called Life*
- **#7** *Gentlemen of the Shade. My Own Private Idaho*
- **#8** *Ain't No Place for a Hero. Borderlands*
- **#9** *Most Dramatic Ever. The Bachelor*
- **#10** *Let's Go Exploring. Calvin and Hobbes*
- **#11** *Extra Salty. Jennifer's Body*
- **#12** *Right, Down + Circle. Tony Hawk's Pro Skater*
- **#13** *The Time of My Life. Dirty Dancing*
- **#14** *Clever Girl. Jurassic Park*
- **#15** *Ugh! As If! Clueless*
- **#16** *It Can't Rain All the Time. The Crow*

# it can't rain all the time.
## the crow
## alisha mughal

ecwpress

Copyright © Alisha Mughal, 2025

Published by ECW Press
665 Gerrard St. East
Toronto, Ontario, Canada M4M 1Y2
416-694-3348 / info@ecwpress.com

All rights reserved. No part of this publication may be reproduced, stored in a retrieval system, or transmitted in any form by any process — electronic, mechanical, photocopying, recording, or otherwise — without the prior written permission of the copyright owners and ECW Press. The scanning, uploading, and distribution of this book via the Internet or via any other means without the permission of the publisher is illegal and punishable by law. This book may not be used for text and data mining, AI training, and similar technologies. Please purchase only authorized electronic editions, and do not participate in or encourage electronic piracy of copyrighted materials. Your support of the authors' rights is appreciated.

Editor for the press: Jen Sookfong Lee
Copy editor: Carrie Gleason
Cover and text design: David Gee

Library and Archives Canada Cataloguing in Publication

Title: It can't rain all the time : The crow / Alisha Mughal.

Other titles: It cannot rain all the time | Crow

Names: Mughal, Alisha, author.

Series: Pop classic series ; #16.

Description: Series statement: Pop classics ; 16 | Includes bibliographical references.

Identifiers: Canadiana (print) 20250167379 | Canadiana (ebook) 20250167387

ISBN 978-1-77041-818-9 (softcover)
ISBN 978-1-77852-408-0 (ePub)
ISBN 978-1-77852-409-7 (PDF)

Subjects: LCSH: Crow (Motion picture : 1994) | LCSH: Mughal, Alisha. | LCSH: Emotions in motion pictures.

Classification: LCC PN1997.C76 M84 2025 | DDC 791.43/72—dc23

Printing: Friesens   5   4   3   2   1
PRINTED AND BOUND IN CANADA

This book is funded in part by the Government of Canada. Ce livre est financé en partie par le gouvernement du Canada. We acknowledge the support of the Canada Council for the Arts. Nous remercions le Conseil des arts du Canada de son soutien. We acknowledge the funding support of the Ontario Arts Council (OAC), an agency of the Government of Ontario. We also acknowledge the support of the Government of Ontario through the Ontario Book Publishing Tax Credit, and through Ontario Creates.

Purchase the print edition and receive the ebook free. For details, go to ecwpress.com/ebook.

For Evee

## Contents

Introduction 9

## Part One: Literal Death

The Author, the Graphic Novel, the Grief 21

Interlude I 49

The Actor, the Film, the Inevitable Death 54

## Part Two: Visceral Life

Breathed to Life 101

Interlude II 136

Continued Breath 138

Conclusion 155

Sources 159

Acknowledgments 165

**Introduction**

A depressive episode begins as a slow and steady sinking feeling, like being lowered inch by inch into a grave. I feel it build over the course of a couple of days or sometimes even a week. I grow irritable, and my moods begin to turn putrid as negative thoughts lay roots. As my body grows tired, the thoughts become a forest. The episode has set in.

When I was younger, I was consumed by the muck of sadness, and many times, I almost didn't make it out. Now I'm on medication, which doesn't completely stop the episodes but does allow me a remove, a distance from which I can make decisions to help myself. I've learned that the only thing I can do is to let these episodes play out, allow them to peak and then fade and then, eventually, recede. This takes time. Sometimes I watch movies as the hours pass.

The first time I watch *The Crow* is during a depressive episode at the beginning of the summer I turn 29. Scrolling through the horror streaming platform Shudder, I see the film's poster image one empty evening. It's still light out, and I hear sounds that never fail to make me feel like the loneliest person in the world: people laughing, children playing. I vaguely recall the film's association with some kind of catastrophe, which I learned about from online critic Marya E. Gates years ago. In the state that I'm in in my darkening bedroom — my eyes sore and my mouth feeling like it's stuffed with cotton balls — I can't recall much else about the film.

As I'm staring numbly at the screen, my sleepy attention is piqued by the poster's suffocating darkness stained with the red gash of a title: it's a heavy black relieved only by the lead actor's name and a steely gray-white light, like a doorway just opened onto something magnificent. "Believe in angels," the film's tagline, framed in the light, advises. On the threshold, a small and menacing figure is visible as if in relief, his arms hang as a sentence cut short, flexed at his sides, making him look like a panther about to pounce — he is as dark as the velvety black on the poster's body. He is walking toward the viewer, perennially. It is a moody image, sinister and gothic, and, on this empty evening, it complements my melancholic insides, so I press play.

A horror overcomes me. I see Brandon Lee's Eric Draven lying dead on the street after being thrown from his apartment window and then crawling his way out of a muddy grave moments later, screaming and wailing from the pain of a macabre rebirth. When I hear Eric speak for the first time in the movie — he whispers his cat's name, Gabriel — his voice low and gravelly from the strain of life so recently shocked into him, I turn the film off and weep. I can't finish it. Not yet.

Lee's stature, his voice, his rain-sodden hair — it all reminds me of a person I am trying very hard to forget. "It hurts to watch because you look so much like him," I say when I manage to see him a few weeks later, the first time in a year. The Boy I Was Trying to Forget isn't exactly the direct cause of my sadness. It's my own unreciprocated and unbearably heavy feelings for him that leave me feeling unmoored, which then feed into the loneliness that characterizes my depressive episodes. Everything becomes so dire, so tangled, because of and within my mind.

It might seem anticlimactic or boring or unimportant, maybe even anti-feminist, to say that my fascination with *The Crow* was first sparked by a man who didn't like me back. But it's the truth.

Later that summer, it finally dawns on me that he, the person whose loss I ought to be able to deal with, would never change his mind about me. And it is only at this point, when I understand that my hope will not be enough, that I will have to deal with the finality of his indifference to me — that I sit myself down and watch *The Crow* in its entirety.

And then I watch it again, and again, and again. Every night that I am sad and weeping, every night that I feel as lonely and meaningless as a lace handkerchief lost at sea (so much elaborate intricacy, so much feeling, all wasted), I put it on. The first time I visit one of my dearest friends in San Francisco, I talk her into watching it with me. It is her first time. We suck gin gimlets through puckered lips, and I become teary-eyed watching Eric Draven twirl and charge and weep and wail.

Now two years have gone by, and I've come to realize that I turned to *The Crow* so often that first summer because it was a way to avoid reality, a way to avoid countenancing and mourning and moving on from the end of a connection. The film allowed me closeness with a person who was far away and would never come near. He wasn't dead, but this was worse, I once thought with self-pitying conviction. When a loved one dies, you at least have the assurance that there had been love. But this, of course, was a false comparison; it is objectively not preferable to lose someone to death. Still, that certainty I once felt was deeply, pleasingly maudlin, a kind of gothic romanticism. Just like everything I love about *The Crow*.

\*

Directed by Alex Proyas, *The Crow* is based on a graphic novel of the same name by James O'Barr. It was released in 1994 after a fraught production period beleaguered by time constraints, delays, and mishaps. Hurricanes tumbled through the miniature city Proyas had built, crew members suffered accidents, and, most notably, lead actor Brandon Lee died on set due to a misfired, misloaded, and mishandled prop gun. During filming, in the face of so many accidents, many on set thought the film was cursed.[1] It was well-received by critics, with nearly everyone noting the irony of a lead actor dying during production for a film about a character brought back from the dead. Roger Ebert stated that Lee's performance is "more of a screen achievement than any of the films of his father, Bruce Lee."[2] The critical consensus on *Rotten Tomatoes* is that the film is "filled with style and dark, lurid energy," and that it carries "a soul in the performance of the late Brandon Lee."[3]

It made a lot of money, was considered a sleeper hit at the box office, and spawned three standalone sequels that are, honestly, very terrible. Today, the film has a devoted cult following. At screenings, some fans dress up as Eric Draven, painting their faces black and white and caping their bodies in a glossy black flowing trench coat. Sometimes, they adhere a prop crow to their shoulder in honor of the talismanic animal that serves as a shepherd and guide and spiritual conduit for Eric's soul. There are some critics, though, who wonder whether this movie would still have a devoted following were it not for the real-life tragedy.

The first time I saw the film in a theater, some audience members laughed during scenes that, to me, were never very funny. At one point, Eric, after arming himself with all manner of weapons at a pawn shop (where he also recovers his dead

---

[1] "The Crow," IMDb, accessed May 3, 2024, https://www.imdb.com/title/tt0109506/trivia/?item=tr2585918&ref_=ext_shr_lnk.

[2] Roger Ebert, "Reviews: The Crow," movie review and film summary, RogerEbert.com, May 13, 1994, https://www.rogerebert.com/reviews/the-crow-1994.

[3] "The Crow," Rotten Tomatoes, accessed May 3, 2024, https://www.rottentomatoes.com/m/the_crow.

fiancée's ring), picks up an electric guitar. The unplugged guitar moans: its strings, as Eric carries it away, vibrate, creating a ghostly *boing-oing-oing*. Watching the film with an audience, I could see how that scene, the juxtaposition of guns with a guitar, could seem a bit funny — a man arming himself ahead of battle takes only the most important things. Surely a guitar is a bit too extravagant? But at the same time, I wanted to shush everyone. Couldn't they see that the guitar is important to Eric, a musician, just as much as the ring? To laugh is to misunderstand Eric, for whom nothing is trivial or extravagant, and everything is significant. People laughed nonetheless, and at other moments, too, when things became a bit clunky and ludicrous.

"Very bizarre situations are often darkly funny," said supporting cast member David Patrick Kelly in a behind-the-scenes interview for *The Crow*,[4] reinforcing that the wry humor was purposeful and necessary. The film was pieced together under traumatic circumstances, and this sometimes comedic overwrought-ness is central to its ethos. *The Crow* is all about a romantic and melancholic pain like an exposed nerve, which the film prods and pokes with the same macabre curiosity that prompts us to press on a tender bruise and can also make us laugh in discomfort or dismay.

In *The Crow*, there is a pain that is too much; it throbs and glistens with lifeblood, even in and around so much death, appearing on characters in ways that rail against logic's

---

4 "Behind the Scenes «The Crow» (1994)," YouTube, January 27, 2017, https://www.youtube.com/watch?v=hmaimTyH56g.

expectations. The curious thing is that, although this heavy darkness is easy to slip into when sad, it's not an easy watch precisely for this heft. The film's pain ricochets through me during every one of my rewatches, reawakening and corralling to the surface all my own fanged memories, which can be, in a sort of paradox, a celebration of life. Pain is messy, emotions are gooey, and they bleed into one another. But ultimately, and most importantly, tears, fear, laughter, and grief are signs that we are *alive*, a truth that *The Crow* is a brave and relentless reminder of.

*

When I first meet The Boy, I can't imagine how I got so lucky. He shows me kindness and attention, he sees me fully, and he holds me in moments that my body remembers long afterward. And when he breaks the news to me that he isn't looking for anything serious, that this has just been a fling, it is incomprehensible. How can something mean nothing? My desire for life and love is met in a magical instant, and then it is unmet just as swiftly. Having tasted bliss, I feel even lonelier than before.

I tell you this because the first time I watched *The Crow*, I could see an intensity of emotion that mirrored my own. *It's okay to feel this intensely about something sad that happened*, this film seems to say. Through it, I see my maudlin-ness as something allowed, something being depicted without shame. *The Crow*, like so much art, is a kind guide through the complications of our souls. James O'Barr, Eric Draven, and me — the three of us are together during every viewing and, somehow, we are less beleaguered, a parasocial trifecta of emotional peace.

*

*The Crow* is *actually* a good movie: a meaningful work of art unto itself. This is a work of art borne of tragedy, which also ended up birthing tragedy. At the same time, *The Crow*, embedded so deeply within its historical context, transcends its literal tragedies because of its universal emotionality. The counterculture of the early '90s, captured by the film's grungy visual aesthetic and sonic landscape, is everywhere. Characters shoot heroin wearing torn fishnets and bleary eye makeup. They sport tangled undercuts, chokers, and Doc Martens. Music by The Cure, Nine Inch Nails, and Stone Temple Pilots keeps time in a sleepless city, an urban symbol of idealism's decay. But even as the film is rooted firmly in the era, Eric's grief is an ancient one. His feelings of sadness and anger tower to biblical heights and resonate with anyone who's ever felt loss. This is the film's timeless soul, something impossible to capture by any paint-by-numbers sequel.

The film is often seen as gaining its poignancy from Lee's death, but I would argue that it has a soul on a level distinct from the tragedies that loom over it. This is a good film, and there is also tragedy here; it is not "good" *because* there is tragedy here. It is viscerally human and emotional.

Film scholar Carol J. Clover writes that most horror films are clichéd, working from a handful of folktales that have haunted us for ages. A film's quality as a work of art lies not so much in whether it has some new knowledge to gift us but in how, during "the art of rendition or performance," it delivers the cliché, or the familiar and human.[5] Most good art communicates something viscerally true about life and the human condition; a good film makes us fearful or sad or hopeful because its soul finds something in ours to resonate with. *The Crow* is as Clover describes: it manages to deliver something old, something that we have been grappling with for ages — death and its attendant, grief — through an exceedingly particular rendition, locked in time.

This book is divided into two sections, charting the two ways the film delivers its "cliché," which is not something trite but something eternally human. The first section is called "Literal Death," and it describes the time-bound particularities of *The Crow*'s production — all the literal deaths that surround the story. This first section maps out the *how*, the artifice, the work it took to create *The Crow*, both the graphic novel and the film, work that centers death. The second part is called "Visceral Life," and it illuminates the story's beating heart, sketching the topography of the film's themes of grief and love.

*The Crow* is known for the death surrounding its production, but it could just as well be infamous for the life it allows. Creating art and interacting with it as viewers can often lead to healing. This film transcends death with its everlasting life in precisely this way, continuing to weep, love, and hope. The

---

[5] Carol J. Clover, *Men, Women, and Chain Saws: Gender in the Modern Horror Film* (Princeton University Press, 1992).

story preserves both James O'Barr's and Eric's grieving processes, like snow globes that come to life when we need them to.

In watching *The Crow*, I learn something crucial. Despite all the deaths, literal and narrative, there is so much life here. How else could Eric, suffering as much as he does, so persistently and staunchly believe that "It can't rain all the time," a lyric he once wrote in his previous life as a musician? The back-from-the-dead Eric repeats this to Sarah, a child and friend who has become as lonely as he is. Eric has hope. And through him, *The Crow*, this film defined by tragedy, shows us how to build a hope like Eric's, which is, of course, necessary for life.

# part one
# literal death

# 1

## The Author, the Graphic Novel, the Grief

JAMES O'BARR

Artist and author James O'Barr is quiet when he talks.

In *A Profile of James O'Barr*, the 30-minute intimate interview conducted in 2000 for *The Crow*'s "Collector's Series," O'Barr sits sketching in the basement of his home in Detroit, a cigarette hanging out the side of his mouth. He doesn't make much eye contact with the camera, looking up toward the ceiling or down to the ground as he combs through his past to tell his story, the whole of it — before, during, and after *The Crow*.

What emerges is a full life, dimensional, tough, and happy, all in, perhaps, unequal measure. What emerges is the totality of a complex man, a totality of facts that lends much more meaning and nuance to his creation, Eric.

The graphic novel's plot is simultaneously fairly straightforward and contorted like an artery. Eric — *just* Eric, without a last name — is a mechanic, but this is not too important. What is important is that which gives meaning to Eric's life and makes him blessed among the unblessed: his love, Shelly. She is all that Eric cares about, and she feels the same way. She is madly and dizzily in love with Eric. One night, after the two have celebrated their engagement, in a freak turn of fate, they are attacked by a gang of Detroit's most horrifying: Tin Tin, Fun Boy, T-Bird, Top Dollar, and Tom Tom.

Shelly dies on site after being raped by each of the gang members. Eric, shot in the head and body several times, survives for a few hours and is taken to hospital, where he undergoes emergency surgery but eventually succumbs to his injuries. A crow visits Eric while he is teetering on the edge of consciousness, apparently there to shepherd him into the afterlife. (An interesting theory on the IMDb page for the film version of *The Crow* states that much of the book's ensuing violence is a revenge fantasy Eric has while he's comatose, but I wonder if this is too uninspired a reading, sapping the book of its heartbreaking vigor and immediacy, of its magic and hope.)[6]

A year after the murders, Eric is brought back to life by the same crow. In mythology, the crow is a powerful figure — in

---

[6] "The Crow," IMDb, accessed May 3, 2024, https://www.imdb.com/title/tt0109506/trivia/?item=tr0697493&ref_=ext_shr_lnk.

many cases, they represent interjections by divinity, acting as messengers.[7] According to author A.A. Attanasio, who writes the 1992 afterword to *The Crow*, the corvid appears in mythology across cultures the world over, each time serving as a powerful pro-generative force, as a god or goddess-like entity: "The crow is the hunger of the sky," he writes.[8]

In O'Barr's book, The Crow is Eric's celestial guide but also an observer and a sarcastic judge. Functioning as a culvert between the divine and mortal, The Crow in the book provides Eric with counsel and guidance but also winces at his pain, even as he shepherds him through it. Sometimes, as Eric walks through the house he shared with Shelly, The Crow, almost like a sardonic sorcerer or a bewitching trickster, prompts the resurfacing of memories that singe and sear. They veritably burn as they lick Eric in all his most tender parts.

"You were closest here, weren't you?" The Crow says as Eric stares into his and Shelly's bedroom in a mini-chapter called "Watching Forever."[9]

"Remember the smell of her hair?"[10]

In one of the mini-chapter's final panels, Eric clasps his hands over his ear and grimaces, his face awash with tears, as

---

[7] Patti Wigington, "The Magic of Crows and Ravens in Mythology," Learn Religions, July 19, 2024, https://www.learnreligions.com/the-magic-of-crows-and-ravens-2562511#:~:text=For%20the%20ancient%20Greeks%2C%20the,direction%20from%20which%20it%20flew.

[8] James O'Barr, *The Crow* (Gallery 13, 2017).

[9] Ibid.

[10] Ibid.

if doing this might stop the noise of his memories that The Crow prompts.

"Why do you do this to yourself?" The Crow asks over his shoulder, suddenly distancing from Eric and morphing like a trickster from shepherd to judge. It's an impossible question to answer because painful memories, once triggered, have a knack of rolling into view with a forceful inevitability. The Crow's words echo that familiar inner dialogue we have all experienced when we are stuck in painful memories, simultaneously holding up the past and chastising ourselves for looking in their direction.

Eric has spent the year roiling in a liminal space between heaven and hell, wracked by his guilt and grief at not having saved Shelly, even as this guilt is unfounded. He couldn't have helped her, and he did try. The Crow is sent down to the beleaguered Eric, who is given the opportunity of resurrection, and stays by Eric's side while the momentarily immortal young man fulfills the singular goal that he hopes might allay his soul: the punitive murder of his murderers. O'Barr's story, however, ends on a barbed realization for Eric: externally directed revenge is no tonic for a soul restless with misplaced guilt. "The resolution isn't about justice or revenge," The Crow tells Eric after he has killed everyone responsible for his and Shelly's deaths but finds himself still wandering the mortal plane. "It's about forgiveness." When Eric says he could never forgive his killers, The Crow calls him an idiot: "Not them, yourself! If you want to leave this in-between place, you have to let it go." Eric must forgive himself for not being able to save Shelly.

✱

In *A Profile of James O'Barr*, even when O'Barr raises his voice to ask his wife to be quiet for filming, his tenor never lands above a calm and steady register.

"You telling me to shut up?" his wife asks from somewhere out of view; you can sense a playful grin in her tone.[11] The person behind the camera laughs.

"I'm telling you not to be banging shit around or turning the TV on," O'Barr says. It's evident he's enjoying the mock quarrel they're playing out for the camera. Indeed, it seems sweet, saccharine, like something out of one of the flashbacks in *The Crow*. A token of true, blissful love. The short documentary begins with this banter and ends with O'Barr looking forward to exciting developments in his family. O'Barr has had a tough life, but he is happy now. In a sense, this interview begins and ends with an assurance that hope is worthwhile.

The interviewer, Jennifer Peterson, is never seen or heard, but she has clearly asked O'Barr to lay out not only the trajectory of his life, all that has marked or marred it, but also his creative philosophy. His even tone doesn't indicate that he is indifferent to the events that make up his life. Rather, it seems as though he has worked through them and has accepted, processed, and grown from them. As he talks about his life, he holds himself accountable, noting, for example, if he responds to certain tragedies with unhealthy coping

---

[11] Alex Proyas, director, *The Crow*, Miramax, 2020.

mechanisms or when he offers grace to his parents, understanding their socioeconomical experience and their subsequent attitudes toward his art.

In many of the interviews I've read that feature O'Barr, he is nothing but frank, and once one learns his philosophy and has read *The Crow*, it becomes evident that O'Barr has no need, nor any desire, to be anything but honest.

"I'm not a typical comic book artist," he says to Peterson. Some artists illustrate others' stories, but this isn't the case for O'Barr — for most of the works he's produced, he has been both writer and illustrator. This is because, he says, his art and stories do not merely come from him, but they *need* to come from him. "It has to have some kind of a personal attachment for me to be involved in it because it takes so much out of me to do this."

O'Barr, who says he started drawing as soon as his little hands could hold a crayon, is drawing throughout much of the interview; when we don't see the pencil in his hand flitting over the white drawing paper on his desk, we hear it, its dry scrawls carving away, working frenetically to transcribe an image in his mind. "Every single line on that paper comes from me, and every single line is there for a purpose," he says. "None of it is just eye candy. Everything has a meaning there. And because it's so draining and it takes so much out of me, something has to be worthwhile for me to invest that much emotion into it." All of the projects he has completed, he says, have contained, in a sense, a literal and figurative personal statement.

"Nothing has been for pure entertainment value," he says. Many of his projects, and *The Crow* stands towering among them in this case, have functioned as therapy, excising his feelings onto the page so that his anger and frustrations might stop torturing him, so that he might countenance them and work through them. "It was a lot cheaper than seeing a therapist," he says with his eyebrows raised, matter-of-factly.

O'Barr was, in his words, born in a trailer sometime between Christmas and New Year's 1960 in Detroit, and because his birth mother couldn't remember his date of birth, he was assigned January 1 as his birthday. He lived in the foster care system until he was adopted at the age of seven. As a kid, finding the stencils in children's coloring books to be lackluster, he would draw his own images and then color them in. Because he hardly said a word amongst his foster families and avoided interacting with them — most of the foster homes he was placed in were not good situations — he started expressing himself through art.

O'Barr has not had any formal art training. He taught himself most of what he knows about his craft, learning the human form's anatomy from High Renaissance sculptor and painter Michelangelo. Another of O'Barr's influences has been Will Eisner, a pioneering cartoonist who was one of the first to work in the periodical form of the American comic book style.[12] Particularly, it was Eisner's series entitled *The Spirit*, which ran from 1940 to 1952, that affected O'Barr.

The Spirit is the alias of a private detective named Denny Colt who, after dying in the pursuit of a bad guy, is brought back from the grave to fight crime as a masked avenger. The

---

12 Simon Bird, "The Crow: The Graphic Novel," Thecrow.info, 1998, archived September 16, 2016, https://web.archive.org/web/20160916202142/http://www.thecrow.info/granovel.htm.

Spirit doesn't possess any meaningful superpowers, though the fact of his resurrection lends him an aura of the supernatural, and he uses his hard-boiled wit and brute strength to overpower criminals. The series strikes closer to brooding noir than other traditional superhero comics. The Spirit has a very human form: he is not outlandishly muscular, though he does cut a traditional masculine figure, and he is unsmiling in an existentially fraught manner, sidling around corners and lurking in smoky blue shadows, surrounded by grit and sultry scum. He looks to me a lot like Raymond Chandler's Philip Marlowe.

The Spirit scans as a rudimentary but distinct inspiration for Eric in terms of gloomy style (The Spirit's noir bent is carried in Eric's sardonic, Marlowe-esque wit) and resurrection. Both The Spirit and Eric are human beings granted a moment of immortality to avenge wrongdoing. While Eric has a personal stake in the bad guys he hunts, he, like The Spirit, uses his natural abilities and the tools his surroundings provide to carry out his aims, and, distinct from traditional superheroes, Eric bleeds and cries and feels pain. Just as The Spirit is, effectively, an immortal cop, Eric is an immortal sad boy, his vengeful wrath given the gift of deathlessness.

According to O'Barr, traditional comics that depict superheroes contain an exaggeration of the human form. Lacking in weight and solidity, lacking context or embeddedness in space and time, superheroes are the idealized human, godlike, and often, as they clean up after humans, they are above the sweat and drudgery of everyday life, unaffected by the laws of physics as they fly through the sky. O'Barr doesn't recommend looking to traditional comics if one is just beginning to draw, as they are twice removed from the mess of life, from the contradictory way the wind whips hair about to the way fright or rage contorts one's face in ugly ways. According to O'Barr, it's important to have a grounding in real life, which is the source material of all source materials, and an understanding of the human form before one goes about challenging or exaggerating it.

*The Crow*, more than anything, is human and earthly.

THE GRAPHIC NOVEL

O'Barr's figures in *The Crow* are beautiful beings because of his skill, but they are also deeply and obviously *human*. Characters are muscular, but muscles closer to the rangy, sinewy kind gained from a tough life — addiction, violence done to others or the self, hunger, grief — rather than absurd and bulging. O'Barr has a deft understanding of the workings of the human body, especially how it strains under dire socioeconomic circumstances: how skin and muscle tense and snap from fear as much as from physical impact, how stomachs bulge from hunger, how tears sometimes stream like blood. The grit within *The Crow*'s pages is base and earthly, and unabashedly so.

If every one of O'Barr's ink strokes serves a purpose, and if *The Crow* contains all of the author and artist's anguish, then the book is an awe-inspiring thing. Eric's external world is captured by O'Barr with the keen perception of a landscape artist. Much of the setting is a faithful depiction of the Detroit O'Barr walked through, with many of the characters aside from the protagonist based on real people, their names inspired by graffiti O'Barr saw around the city. Eric and all those who meet his wrath are similarly presented with the lyrical perspicuity of a classically trained painter or sculptor: all those feelings, thoughts, and movements that fester and lurk in societal and psychic underbellies are visually manifested. In other words, O'Barr has us countenance the verboten, whether it's personal or societal, through artwork that is jarring and jolting, emphasizing the ugly we all literally and figuratively contain.

Eric's world is dirty, wet, dark, poor, and ruthless, peopled by misfits and outlaws and their victims. O'Barr shows bodies shaking from withdrawal, noses running alongside tears. He visually takes us through the process of pulling morphine from a glass bottle into a syringe. Eric's playground is hideous: dilapidated bars are littered with cigarette packs and the ashy remains of matches, and garbage-lined alleys are picked over by stray cats as rainwater runs in greasy rivulets down cracks in the sidewalk. Eric makes his world uglier with his violence, staining it with his own and others' blood, marking it with bullet casings and holes, adding blood to the slatey rainwater.

When Eric and Shelly, who just pages earlier glimmer with beauty and happiness, are murdered, we see the trail Tin Tin's bullet leaves in Eric's face as it blinds one eye, scars the bridge of his nose, and finally becomes lodged in the side of his mouth. We see blood dripping from half of Shelly's lifeless face (the other half was blown away because she was screaming too much) as Fun Boy assaults her dead body, his bare ass exposed as he stumbles with his pants around his ankles. And with the same unflinching gaze that O'Barr directs at physical, geographical, and societal viscera, he focuses in on psychological darkness, conveying an earth-shattering grief when Eric paints the couple's former home with blood that drips from his self-harm.

O'Barr's bodies make messes. There is a lot of blood in *The Crow* — it spurts and splatters, sprays as bullets enter heads, graffities walls, and bulges in skulls when it can't escape. The book's final pages are a visual symphony of violence. O'Barr uses deft techniques to have us linger over the thrash and clang of bodies being mutilated by Eric's wrath, bodies that include Eric's.

"You can't really guide the reader in how much time to spend on each picture when he's reading the story," O'Barr tells Peterson. "To slow a page down, you have to put more panels in it, more pictures, so they have to spend more time reading it. Put more dialogue or more caption balloons on a page to keep them on the page longer. If you want to speed it up, you use big panels like on the action sequences."

The effect of O'Barr's careful control of pacing in the book's final pages results in an overwhelming feeling of ache as we witness the havoc Eric brings to the evildoers in Detroit, a testament to O'Barr's skill. Certain panels linger over Eric's body but do not exalt his physique, which O'Barr is careful to show as something earned (punctuating Eric's sprees are panels depicting the effort he takes to work out and ready himself for his battles). Rather, O'Barr asks us to observe the violence done to it: the bullet holes, the scars, the crown of thorns Eric has carved into his own chest with a knife.

O'Barr would work and work at capturing the human form in its textured fallibility, he says, focusing on parts of the body until he felt satisfied, until he felt he could capture any aspect of the body in any position or movement and maintain a resemblance to reality. In other words, "make it do what I needed it to do to tell a story," he tells Peterson. Throughout *The Crow*, there are pages after pages, panels after panels that depict an unspeaking Eric, sitting, languishing, thrashing, self-mutilating, dancing, always moving or visibly *feeling*, beat by beat, on the page, telling his story with no words at all.

### THE YOUNG ARTIST AND HIS HEART

"Believe it or not, I got a failing grade in art class," O'Barr says in the documentary, noting he had a "foolish" high school art instructor who stuck so closely to the curriculum that he left no curiosity wiggle room among his students. "Not to sound arrogant or anything, but I was so far ahead of everyone else that their typical assignments were just things that I had done when I was a toddler. I could not bring myself to do that. I was doing these big epic scenarios while everybody else was drawing a cone."

Further barriers to his artistic endeavors were O'Barr's adoptive parents. His father was a bus driver who earned $2.30 per hour. Because of their economic position, his parents highly valued observable labor that was repaid in wages. As a teenager, O'Barr was forbidden from drawing at home because his parents saw it as the equivalent of playing cards, so they forced him to get a job. "They didn't see art as any type of a career," he says. "It was just a hobby to waste time with."

He took on a series of jobs, like washing dishes at a restaurant and working at a retirement home, but never stopped drawing. At school or at the library, O'Barr continued to work on his craft, and it became a secret from his parents.

O'Barr says that up until he met Beverly at the age of 16, he felt his life was a test of endurance, that life was throwing every possible misfortune his way and waiting to see whether he would succumb or survive. "I felt like God had his elbow on my neck my whole life," he says. Beverly was The Girl Who Was Shelly, the girl who changed O'Barr's life. He saw her as an angel, "a bright white light" or a "shining light." "For fighting through that 16 years of difficulty, I finally got to the end and I got the prize." He notes that the book faithfully depicts Beverly as he saw her, even keeping her '70s shag.

Though O'Barr's artwork abounds in depictions of unrelenting violence that maintains its very real ugliness, there is also delicate and hazy beauty. Shelly appears in the book just as O'Barr describes Beverly, all white light and love. While Eric is deep scars of black ink, Shelly is its absence: her skin is an unblemished canvas for Eric's lips. The only black ink used on her face is in her dark lashes and the crimson of her lips.

Shelly's beauty and Eric's memories of her are jarring, harrowing amongst the violence that Eric unleashes. Even as the two are beautiful in their romance, Eric's memories are heartbreaking in their perfection. How could so much beauty be lost? One of Eric's most heartbreaking memories is something prosaically romantic juxtaposed with something violent: Eric jumps into the bath that Shelly is enjoying, and they make love; on the next page begins "The Atrocity Exhibition," which graphically depicts the violent night they were murdered.

Shelly represents a paradise lost.

When O'Barr talks about his relationship with Beverly, it's almost unreal, like something out of a classic romance tale. He often describes her as radiance and divine intervention incarnate. "If I would verbally attack someone, she would point out their good side," he says. "It was like positive and negative; we just fit together perfect." He spent every waking moment with her for three years, and they were engaged to be married after graduation. In the documentary, his brows furrow and he begins fidgeting. He has gotten to the part in his story that many must be familiar with by now, the part that landmarks his life.

O'Barr was 19 and hadn't paid his car insurance, so he called Beverly and asked her to pick him up one night, telling her he couldn't afford to get another ticket. Beverly, of course, agreed: "It was one of those moments when your life suddenly turns sideways for no goddamned good reason . . . a series of choices that trip and fall like dominoes, ending in irreversible consequences," O'Barr writes in the introduction to the book's special edition. Beverly headed to her car to pick him up, but she never made it. A drunk driver struck her, killing her instantaneously. O'Barr held himself responsible: "If I'd only paid my car insurance . . . if I'd only waited ten more minutes to call . . . if I'd only said, 'I'll just see you tomorrow, punkin!' If, if, if," he laments.[13]

Struck by the most incapacitating grief and sadness, O'Barr writes that he could see no future for himself, could see nothing on his horizon "but nothingness." It is this incident that integrally inspired the story of *The Crow*: a beautiful and all-consuming love violently destroyed. It is Beverly and her loss that charges through the book, animating each of the strokes and scrawls, the anguish over her loss so deeply ingrained into the work that you can feel it if you run your fingers over the ink. "If there was no justice in the real world, I would invent some," O'Barr writes.

But, of course, revenge and justice aren't ever powerful enough to assuage self-directed guilt. Accordingly, the book's special edition contains a "new" closing segment called "Sparklehorse" that follows Eric after he has killed the men responsible for his and Shelly's murders. O'Barr added it in

---

13 James O'Barr, *The Crow* (Gallery 13, 2017).

2010 after his newfound (at the time) realization that "forgiveness is for the forgiver."

In "Sparklehorse," Eric is confronted by a horse that appears at the beginning of the original edition of *The Crow* while he is sitting in a purgatorial train for the year between his death and rebirth. Eric waves at the horse from the train and thereby distracts it. The creature looks at him with gleaming, kind eyes. With its head turned toward Eric, it doesn't see a barbed-wire fence coming up ahead, and it runs into it headlong. The fence mangles and slashes and kills the horse. Eric is horrified with himself, holding himself responsible; if only he hadn't waved at the horse.

The horse reappears in "Sparklehorse" with its mane a literal blaze of whirling fire. After killing T-Bird, Eric is walking through a forest. He hasn't been immediately reunited with Shelly in the peaceful finality of death, which he expected. The Crow is perched on his shoulder. The two have just discussed what resolution entails, and The Crow tells Eric that he needs to simply "let it go" if he wants to leave his in-between state. The horse then appears wrapped up in the barbed wire that killed it and is whinnying and thrashing with wild eyes. "What do I have to do?" Eric asks, forlorn and tired. The Crow suggests one of the many weapons he is armed with. Eric pulls out a gun and shoots the horse square in its head, putting it out of its misery.

When I was in an outpatient cognitive behavioral therapy program after a failed suicide attempt, we were taught to imagine our bad thoughts as having a corporeal presence. If we wanted to get rid of them, we could pick them up, place them in a box or a glass bottle, and float them away into a great body of water or tie them to helium-filled balloons and watch them leave our orbit. Imagining the physical act of banishing the thoughts is believed to make them easier to control. Eric shooting his guilt in the form of Sparklehorse literally puts him out of his misery, or rather, pulls his misery out of him and destroys it, bringing him the peace and calmness to finally accept death.

Eric is finally free.

O'Barr added "Sparklehorse" only after the idea of self-forgiveness dawned on him:

> I always wanted to explore the scene on the train where Eric sees the horse, as it represented his guilt for not being able to help Shelly. I always wanted the horse to be at the end too, but back then I couldn't quite figure out how or why to do it, but twenty years later I fully understand it now . . . It's an intense sequence, but it is a nice wrap-up as it explains that Eric's journey wasn't only about revenge; it was about acceptance. Either you forgive yourself for something, or you let it haunt you for the rest of your life.[14]

I think O'Barr added the scene only after he managed to forgive himself, for Beverly and, later, for Brandon Lee.

---

14 James A. Keith, "James O'Barr on *The Crow*'s 20th Anniversary, His New Project and Dallas," *The Mixmaster*, July 26, 2011, archived February 22, 2014, https://web.archive.org/web/20140222143031/http:/blogs.dallasobserver.com/mixmaster/2011/07/james_obarr_on_the_20th_annive.php.

The specifics around Eric and Shelly's murders are more directly inspired by a news story. "I had read in the newspaper about a couple who were killed over a twenty-dollar engagement ring," O'Barr said in an interview in 2000. "I thought that that was so outrageous that I thought that would be a good typical point for the story to work around."[15] O'Barr named Shelly after Mary Shelley because, just as Shelley creates one of literature's greatest monsters in *Frankenstein*, so had Beverly's death turned O'Barr into a monster, which is why Eric is named after Erik, the Phantom/monster in *The Phantom of the Opera*. "'Shelly's' death had turned me into a monster under my own skin," O'Barr writes in the introduction to his book.[16] When Brandon Lee passed away, O'Barr felt doubly guilty — if only he hadn't written the book that became the film, maybe his friend would still be alive, he notes in the introduction.

Throughout the short documentary, which, absent his wife's voice at the beginning, is mostly O'Barr's face, voice, and sounds of his sketching, Peterson makes the distinct choice to punctuate O'Barr's story chiefly with panels from *The Crow* rather than actual photographs from his past. The effect not only drives home the graphic novel's autobiographical bent but also illustrates his fluid emotions better than any photograph could.

---

15 Philip Anderson, "Interviews: James O'Barr - Author of The Crow," *KAOS2000 Magazine*, July 20, 2000, archived March 23, 2016, https://web.archive.org/web/20160323220745/http://kaos2000.net/interviews/jamesobarr/.

16 James O'Barr, *The Crow* (Gallery 13, 2017).

For the three years following Beverly's death, O'Barr says he engaged in reckless and self-destructive behavior, channeling his grieving anger toward himself. During that period in 1978, he enlisted in the Marines and was stationed in Berlin, Germany. He never stopped making art, working on illustrating combat manuals.

"I finally realized that I was going to have to channel all this into something, or I was going to self-destruct." *The Crow*, he says, was the vehicle that he wanted to carry all his rage and frustration with the world and its tilted justice. "It became my therapy for a long time," he says.

After being discharged from the Marines, he was back in Detroit and working at an auto body shop. Every day after his shift, he came home and worked on *The Crow* until 3 a.m. He refers to his work during this period as "putting in time." He looked to other art, too, specifically music, as he grieved and created. Joy Division was one of the primary influences for *The Crow*, their lyrics even crop up throughout the book. Because O'Barr felt unease with having to draw himself, he modeled Eric after English musician Peter Murphy of the goth-rock group Bauhaus, while Eric's movements were inspired by Iggy Pop. Eric's makeup, meanwhile, his clown paint that the book describes as "the colors of joy," is traditional theater's comedy mask, an irony that casts Eric's pain in stark relief.

## THE GRIEF IN THE GRAPHICS

Eric spends the moments between kills in the home he and Shelly once shared. On his first night back among the living, he sits in their empty living room on a blanket and speaks to himself, to Shelly's ghost, and a cat that he has brought home named Gabriel, a post-mortem birthday surprise for Shelly. In life, she had always said she wanted a cat. As tears stream down his face, he is overcome by the memory of his proposal. It's a memory that wrecks and wracks through Eric — when it has run its course through his body, he lies hunched over, weeping.

O'Barr's Eric wears his feelings unabashedly on his body. When he is sad, he weeps, and when he is angry, he kills. When his memories overwhelm him, he bangs his head against the wall in what is effectively self-harm, an effort to distract his mind with physical pain, the only way he can think of to get his mind to stop replaying the perfume-cloud memories of Shelly.

Later in the book, the memories haunt so ferociously that Eric slashes his forearms with a straight razor, painting a literal image of The Cat in the Hat on the wall with his blood, a grim yet grinning avatar. Eric violently languishes in the house, destroying it and himself little by little until finally burning it down. He is so, so, so tragically sad that even Gabriel seems to weep alongside his scarred and mutilated body. Next to his bloody handprints on the wall, Eric cries and cries, clutching a pillow to his face. "She said, 'Maybe we could make beautiful babies,'" he recalls between sobs. On the subsequent pages,

Eric bandages his arms with electric tape and begins to dance because Shelly liked to dance.

Eric's emotions are visible on his face and on his body, regardless of whether he is alone or amongst others. In front of the thugs he hunts and kills, he vacillates between maniacal laughter and lyrical pathos, tears streaming down his face as he toys with the men like a cat does with mice. O'Barr captures Eric as a man fluidly moved by his roiling mind; his feelings and memories move him and he allows them to. There is an acrobatic grace about Eric. In death, he has become just as swift and nimble as Fred Astaire, as robustly balletic as Gene Kelly, and as raw in his feelings as an Edgar Allan Poe protagonist.

There is a panel about halfway through the book that feels as though it's a black-and-white photograph. It depicts a door at the end of a narrow hallway, and on the wall that abuts it is a bloody handprint, and I can't help but think it must be O'Barr's. His gaze over Eric is deeply personal and enmeshing, as if he is having us bear witness to himself, to his soul. As Eric weeps and wails alone, we feel the heft of O'Barr's hand sketching the images.

In a 1994 interview with *The Boston Phoenix*, O'Barr says:

Writing *The Crow* didn't help at all. I thought it would be cathartic, but as I drew each page, it made me more self-destructive, if anything. There is pure anger on each page, little murders. I was more messed up by the time I was done with the book. There was a rumor going around when there was a delay between the third and fourth issues that I had committed suicide. I was annoyed by that, because God's had his elbow on my neck for this long, I feel I can stick it out. I'm not ready to put a period on that sentence yet.[17]

Yet a moment later, he says that though he wishes he had never written the book (because of Lee's death), if he hadn't written it, he might have died: "I probably wouldn't be here, having been consumed by my very self-destructive behavior."[18] The act of creation, painful though it was, was still a necessary one. In the documentary, he says he could only work on a few pages at a time before he needed to take a break from the sear of the past. Working on 20-page increments, O'Barr took nine years to finish the book. He began it in 1981 and completed it in 1989.

### *THE CROW* AND THE CAREER

By his early thirties, O'Barr felt an itch — he was bored of working on cars, so he, on a whim, applied to medical school and got in. After two years of a very expensive program, he took a sabbatical that he hoped would last a year to work and scrounge up enough money for tuition. One of his jobs was

---

[17] Lisa Susser, "Reliving the Pain," *The Boston Phoenix*, May 13, 1994, archived March 2, 2021, https://archive.org/details/sim_boston-phoenix_may-13-19-1994_23_19/page/n81/mode/2up?view=theater.

[18] Ibid.

creating t-shirts for a comic book store, in whose back room the independent comic publisher Caliber was just taking off.

Gary Reed owned both the retail store O'Barr worked at and Caliber, which specialized in creator-owned books, and was considered in the '90s to be one of America's leading independent comic book publishers.[19] He asked O'Barr if he had any work, and O'Barr showed him *The Crow*, which went on to be one of the first works published by Caliber. The book sold so well that O'Barr found that he was making as much through sales as he was working on cars — he could become a full-time artist. After three issues that sold tremendously well, O'Barr started receiving movie offers.

Something interesting was happening in Hollywood in the late '80s and early '90s. Tim Burton's *Batman* had just been released in 1989 to immense critical and commercial success. Earning more than $400 million at the box office, it became at the time the fifth-highest-grossing film in Hollywood's history, going on to win an Academy Award for Best Art Direction.[20] One of the first truly successful comic book adaptations, the film undoubtedly lit up cartoonish dollar signs in producers' eyes. Its success continues to play a significant hand in Hollywood's attitude toward superhero films.

*Batman*'s success showed producers that superhero or comic-book films could do well, that they had a market. Many were giddy at the prospect and potential, specifically for stories

---

19 "About Us," Caliber Comics, accessed May 3, 2024, https://calibercomics.com/about-us.

20 "Batman," Box Office Mojo, accessed May 3, 2024, https://www.boxofficemojo.com/title/tt0096895/.

that, like *Batman*, had what writer Chris Flackett describes as a "dark heart": "The success of the film proved there was a market for darker comic book films, albeit a darkness tempered by a highly stylised production, an upbeat Prince soundtrack and Jack Nicholson doing what he does best — being Jack Nicholson — as the Joker. Hollywood went scurrying after any comic book it could find with a dark heart it thought it could tame. *The Crow* fit the bill."[21]

"I was really surprised that it didn't take very long for them to latch onto it," O'Barr says in the documentary. But O'Barr did see the potential. "I always saw it as a film. In fact, when I was laying out the pages, I did it in storyboard form."

O'Barr's cinematic vision is apparent in the book's kinetic lens. "When I'm drawing comics, I'm thinking of camera angles," he says. As he draws, he considers where a camera would be placed. "In reality, the camera is just my head." That being said, O'Barr didn't have any film aspirations, and he didn't have much hope that it would ever get made. At one point, O'Barr says a producer thought it might be a good idea to turn *The Crow* into a musical starring Michael Jackson and directed by British documentary and music video director Julien Temple. O'Barr laughed at the suggestion, thinking it was a joke.

"Why did you even buy this thing if you want to completely change it into something unrecognizable?" O'Barr says in the documentary, recalling his feelings when he learned the

---

21 Chris Flackett, "They Keep Calling Me: The Crow's Transference of Trauma into Art," *Film Obsessive*, October 23, 2019, https://filmobsessive.com/film/film-features/film25yl/they-keep-calling-me-the-crows-transference-of-trauma-into-art/.

producer wasn't joking. "Why don't you just come up with your own story?"

Initial production didn't land too far from that one producer's dream: brought on to direct was Australian Alex Proyas in his feature directorial debut. Proyas had worked exclusively and successfully as a music video director. At a time when MTV was seen by record labels as the best way to advertise, Proyas was finding good work: he had worked with INXS and Crowded House and soon found representation with a music video and film production company called Propaganda Films. Eventually, a rudimentary, not very good, version of *The Crow* screenplay came across Proyas's desk, a version that had strayed far from O'Barr's vision. "I spoke to the producer, Ed Pressman, and told him that I didn't like the script so much, but that if I could make it more like the comic book, I'd be really excited to do it," Proyas said in a 2016 interview with Paul Rowlands. "Ed Pressman agreed to that, and we managed to find a writer named David Schow. He and I worked together on the script for a very long period of time until I felt confident we could make a great movie with it."[22]

In Peterson's documentary, O'Barr credits Proyas and Brandon Lee, who joined the project having become a fan of O'Barr's book, for reining the story in, taking it back as close to O'Barr's story as possible. "As far as I'm concerned, Brandon and Proyas are what made the first film," he says. "They're the two real stars of it."

---

22 Paul Rowlands, "An Interview with Alex Proyas (Part 1 of 3)," *Money Into Light*, 2016, https://www.money-into-light.com/2017/01/an-interview-with-alex-proyas-part-1-of.html.

"Back in the '30s, somebody asked Raymond Chandler, 'How do you feel about what Hollywood has done to your books?'" O'Barr says to Peterson. "And he said, 'Fucking Hollywood hasn't done anything to my books. They're right on the shelf where they've always been.' And that's kind of how I think about my stuff, too. It's never going to be what they want it to be. It's never just going to be something pure and entertaining. It's always going to have a personal statement from me."

*

"I'm happier now than I have been since I was 18," O'Barr remarks after saying that though he's 40 (in the interview), he still feels like a teenager. "I'm really glad I didn't decide to just give up and accept things as they were." He finally feels as though he has achieved all he had wanted; he says he can finally enjoy his life. He notes that he doesn't feel like he is being tested anymore or that he is waiting for the good part.

In any piece written about James O'Barr, one would be hard-pressed to find no mention of The Girl Who Was Shelly or the circumstances around *The Crow* or Brandon Lee; there is almost always a mention or suggestion of death and the sadness *The Crow* externalized. But O'Barr seems content at the end of Peterson's interview. He says he finally has hope now, the kind of hope that allows one to populate a future, to extinguish the "nothing . . . but nothingness" on the horizon.[23] For the

---

23 James O'Barr, *The Crow* (Gallery 13, 2017).

first time since Beverly, he feels a love that is just as intense. Strangely, it is not this hope that many touch or end upon when talking about James O'Barr. It is the death, the literal death, and the art inspired by subsequent grief that we, fans of O'Barr's work, can't stop lingering on.

Why is that? When one considers all that O'Barr has survived and all the beauty he has created, why is death the inevitable talking point, what we obsess over? I wonder if the answer is simple. I wonder if it might be because we're looking for instruction, for a map toward hope.

*

In the book, during a conversation with his young friend, Sherri, Eric offers the weeping and terrified child something I have always marveled at: he offers her hope. "I'm sorry," Eric says to Sherri. "I'm sorry for everything that has happened to you, and for everything that is going to happen to you. Please don't be afraid, Sherri. Someday all things will be fair and there will be wonderfull [*sic*] surprises. I truly do believe this."

I've always wondered how Eric could have conceived and vocalized this hope, even after death. I wonder if this advice is O'Barr speaking to himself, mired as he was in the midst of turmoil while crafting his story, grafting his pain onto each stroke of ink only to find that its roots remained within *him*. How is it possible to maintain hope after all that Eric, all that O'Barr, has been through? How is it possible to vocalize it and offer it to another? Does this hope kick in when our bodies realize we're in danger? Because otherwise how could we carry on fighting or surviving? I wonder if this panel is O'Barr showing us that something good can come out of a moment of despair and exhaustion, that the strength of self-made hope is possible when all energy has been sapped by a cruel world.

"See you in heaven, doll," Eric says when he leaves Sherri, and that's pretty well the answer to every question I could ever have about hope.

## INTERLUDE I

I have a hard time with hope.

After graduating from university in 2015, I don't know what to do with myself — I haven't planned to stay alive for this long. I can't get a job — at least, I'm not good at getting one with a philosophy degree. Maybe I don't care enough to try harder. I live at my parents' so I don't have to worry about rent or food and I sleep too much and read too much and start writing short stories. I don't get paid much when some get picked up for publication by independent literary magazines. One editor offers five dollars that he says I can take or let the magazine keep to stay afloat. I let them keep it.

By 2018, I am a few suicide attempts in, and one causes me to check myself into the hospital. A year later, I publish a short story called "Gradual Collapse." It's really creative nonfiction, but I keep that to myself. In the story, I write about how my brain feels "swollen and mushy and dull with pain from the labor of thinking so much and all the time."[24] The story ends with a heavy hospital door slamming onto the middle finger of my left hand (something that really happens as I'm leaving cognitive behavioral therapy), unleashing a pain that surges through my body in thudding waves. Weirdly, I am grateful for this pain and the steely-blue bruise that develops and the swollen way my nail bulges because when I press on

---

24 Catch Business and Elle Nash, eds., *Witch Craft Magazine*, print, vol. 5, 2019.

it, my mind feels like it enters my body. I imagine that Eric's mind pierces through his body when he shreds his forearms and paints his house red with his blood. A physical, momentary break from the sad thoughts.

I first meet The Boy I Was Trying to Forget another year later, in the summer of 2020. I am blindly chasing ways to construct pockets of goodness, ways to give meaning to my life, to give myself something to look forward to, and that pulls my brain out of bad thoughts. But instead of working on building robust and meaningful and lasting friendships, instead of doing the work I learned in cognitive behavioral therapy, because I don't care enough to do it, I look in all the wrong places. I erroneously believe salvation lies in how fit I am for sex: if I am good enough as a sex object, then a man will stay, then I will hold meaning as a human being, then I deserve to exist, and then, maybe, I will put effort into staying alive.

We meet on an app, the flaming bad one. He is an actor, and when I ask him what he's created that he's most proud of, he sends me the link to a short film that is truly very good. I, still relatively fresh out of journalism school and with only a few meaningful bylines, send him the link to a film review. I don't know if he reads it. We agree to meet at a park that I love: nestled deep within a cluster of houses in Toronto's East End, it's a sleepy oasis that unfurls from a flat, lush green field hemmed by thick, tall trees with branches intertwined, protecting the emerald grass like watchful guardians. It can feel like an alcove, the trees eating up any city sounds. On that warm July day, sitting in the dappled shade of a looming tree,

I feel unreal, as though I exist without context, without my sadness, just here and now. It turns out he lives a mere walking distance from this park. What luck.

The day is all powdery yellow, and monarch butterflies suffuse the air. I sit on the ground and spot him when he is still a distance away, walking toward me amidst the hiss of the afternoon summer heat and rippling air, looking like a dream. His shirt is unbuttoned halfway down his torso, and he wears slide-on slippers; I learn he prefers leaving his feet bare, touching the earth. Later in the afternoon, an errant soccer ball rolls our way and he gets up and kicks it back to its owners with his bare feet, and he doesn't wince at all. His skin is pale and hair is long, reaching just to the top of his trapezius muscle, the point where his neck meets his shoulders; it is dark brown like his eyes, which are soft like Gene Kelly's (teddy bear eyes), and falls naturally in loose ringlets, like my own hair. He is tall, six feet and four inches, and lean, very meticulous in caring for his naturally muscular form. And his voice is deep, which makes a sort of sense to me — it must ricochet through all of him, reaching the outside world inevitably in a sonorous bass. His smile is guileless and warm, the kind that always reaches his eyes.

What does surprise me is his artistic sensibility, kindness, and self-awareness. (It's a surprise because many of us, maybe all of us, believe that most beautiful men are dumb.) He models and acts in film and TV and plays, but he also writes poetry and screenplays and songs, and he plays the violin and guitar. We talk for hours that first day, just sit and talk. I don't think anything bad about myself — I am distracted. There is not a single moment of awkward silence, the kind that inevitably expands the first time you meet a person. Talking to him is easy; he feels familiar. We gush at each other about our favorite movies, our likes and dislikes, interjecting when the other says something agreeable or intuitively familiar, redirecting the conversation until another interjection occurs, restarting the cycle.

It seems too good to be true, and it is. I think I'm dating him, and he reveals that he wouldn't use that word about me. So I stop seeing him because I'm looking for something serious: a reason to stay alive. Over the next three years, I meet more people like him who are good distractions in the moment, who I think might offer me some stability, a cure for my loneliness, maybe love. But they never like me enough or they use me and then they leave, and I am alone with myself and my mind again, and it feels like I'm falling into a deep dark hole. I want to stay alive. I want to feel happiness, the fullness of life, but the pockets of goodness always explode, never remain good.

The Boy and I keep returning to each other over the years, and the time we spend together is the best of all my other experiences with men — all bright light like O'Barr's time with and memories of Beverly, like Eric's glimmering time with Shelly. He doesn't yell at me or berate me or push me or humiliate me; we laugh and watch movies. But he always leaves me because he's not looking for anything serious, at least not with me, and I always end up alone and flooded with all the sadness that causes Eric to bash his head against the wall.

I think the pain I inflict on myself — all the times I hit my head, take too many pills, write mean things to myself on my thighs with a ballpoint pen that I dig so deep into my skin it hurts — is a way to distract from the hopelessness that fills my life, in the way that Eric's self-harm distracts. And then I wonder whether The Boy was a positive distraction at all. I thought he portended hope, something to look forward to, something worth living a good life for, in the way that Beverly offered O'Barr hope, in the way Shelly offered Eric meaning. When The Boy and Beverly and Shelly are lost, hope is lost, and a more deleterious distraction comes in to occupy time. Eric begins killing others, and all this destruction is a distraction, and I wonder if it is a negative one, like his self-harm.

But it feels wrong to put the burden of hope onto another person who didn't ask for it. I think I ought to put it on myself. I think, like O'Barr, I should begin with myself.

# 2

## The Actor, the Film, the Inevitable Death

BRANDON LEE

In a behind-the-scenes featurette included on DVD copies of *The Crow*, Brandon Lee manages to steal the show. It's tough to focus on the other cast members or the production team when he delivers his words with all the confidence and gravitas of a born orator. During the interviews with others, I always find myself counting down the seconds until his presence returns.

Watching him speak, it's impossible not to agree with many of the YouTube comments people leave on his interviews, the comments that remark on his eloquence, that say he is so well spoken. His voice is clarion clear, his gaze fixed intently upon the interviewer or in a vague middle ground in front of him as he focuses on his words. He picks up the gist of even the most poorly worded question and responds with generosity at least and enthusiasm at most, as though the interviewer never missed a beat, and he takes his time. He seems kind.

It all seems effortless for him — less like diligent media training and more like his thoughts are coming from him in the moment. Even when the gist of his answers repeats across interviews, he seems to speak with authenticity as if believing in the cause. His eyes flit about like he is searching for the right word order. Clearly, he doesn't speak from a memorized script but from an intuitive knowledge of how to make smooth conversation. An interviewer's dream, he fills awkward pauses, grasping a conversation's trajectory, and, perhaps because it is still early on in his career, he adds information that furthers the dialogue, as opposed to shutting questions down.

In an interview for *Rapid Fire*, Lee's film before *The Crow*, interviewer Jim Whaley stumbles while attempting to communicate that *Rapid Fire* succeeds as an action movie: "It is a dynamic action movie, and for me it's really about as good as — and I don't mean this in a denigrating way at all — this kind of movie can get, because it's — I don't think you would pretend, you know, any more than, uh, a really well-made action film," Whaley finally finishes.[25]

Lee laughs. "That's what we set out to do," he responds to Whaley's rambling thought with a soft smile and a nod of his head, as if he didn't just sit through an awkward delivery of a word salad. "I just try to do my work," he says.

---

[25] "Brandon Lee with Jim Whaley on Cinema Showcase," YouTube, December 4, 2022, https://www.youtube.com/watch?v=J2fNBIj6opM.

The featurette on *The Crow* DVD was filmed to promote the film's release on TV. But after Lee's death in 1993, quotes from it were published in a May 1994 *Entertainment Weekly* article entitled "Brandon Lee's Last Interview," which followed a deeply tender article called "How *The Crow* Flew" by Rebecca Ascher-Walsh. The featurette itself didn't become available until the film's DVD release in the late '90s. Ascher-Walsh's piece is fascinating for the way it presents testimonials from cast and crew and producers: it juxtaposes co-producers Ed Pressman and Jeff Most's diplomatic business speak with the aching words of people who very obviously loved Lee, a subtle condemnation of Hollywood as an opportunistic hound. But more on that later.

In the Whaley interview for *Rapid Fire*, Lee, prompted by a question about how much input he had in the character he plays, offers a wealth of information. He talks about the unique position he was in, the first in his career, of being able to help craft Jake Lo.

"I can't pretend that I wrote any of the script or anything," Lee says. "But I did get the chance to have access to the writer while he was writing it." He goes on to explain that learning a character is like getting to know someone. "This character is interesting in that he finds himself put in a position that he would really rather not be in. And always throughout the script, I kept saying, 'Well why doesn't Jake just go home at this point? Why doesn't Jake just buy a bus ticket and go home at this point?' I kept challenging the writer to come up with credible reasons that he [Jake] would have to be kept there, because left to his own devices, this is not a guy who would want to jump up and say 'Okay, let me help you out!'"

In many of his interviews, especially both the last interview and Ascher-Walsh's piece, Lee emerges as an incandescent force, not only a savvy and hardworking actor with innate curiosity and talent but also a person with immense empathy and a sharp and sardonic wit.

### EARLY YEARS

Brandon Bruce Lee was born on February 1, 1965, in Oakland, California, to legendary martial artist and actor Bruce Lee and Linda Lee Cadwell. He was the eldest of two children. When he was three months old, his family moved to Hong Kong, where he spent his developmental years. His younger sister is Shannon Lee, an actress and martial artist in her own right who works to keep both Bruce's and Brandon's legacies alive.

Brandon Lee was taught martial arts by his father starting from a very young age, "As soon as I could walk," he says in an interview with reporter and critic Bobbie Wygant.[26] "That was kind of how we played at my house." While Bruce was alive, the family split their time between Hong Kong and the U.S.; the family moved permanently to the U.S. when Lee was eight years old, after Bruce's death. Lee grew up speaking Cantonese and attended, according to him, "an all-Chinese

---

26 "Brandon Lee 'Rapid Fire' 7/13/92 - Bobbie Wygant Archive," YouTube, November 7, 2020, https://www.youtube.com/watch?v=u_xX8yw_arY.

school." Wygant asks him in a roundabout way about his mother: "Your mother is American, or . . . ?" She means to ask him if she is white. Lee understands. "She's American," he says with a smile. "She's of Swedish descent," he says quietly.

"As a small boy I traveled all over the place with Dad, appearing on talk shows and performing all sorts of martial arts feats," Lee said in an interview with *People* magazine.[27] He picked up a taste for acting after seeing his father on set. "I've wanted to follow my dad into acting for as long as I can remember."[28] After Bruce's death in 1973, Lee continued his martial arts studies under Dan Inosanto's tutelage, going on to train with Richard Bustillo (Bruce's former student) and Jeff Imada, who was the primary fight choreographer on *The Crow*.

Lee switched from martial arts to soccer after a struggle with expectation and his sense of self — the walls of the spaces he trained in were decorated with pictures of his father, which caused an existential crisis of sorts.[29, 30] He is described variously and vaguely as "troubled" as a teen. The rather sweet article in *People* magazine from 1986, which caught up with Lee swiftly before his first acting endeavor was to air, describes Lee not only

---

[27] "Enter the Son of the Dragon: Bruce Lee's Only Boy, Brandon, Gets No Kick from Kung Fu," *People*, February 3, 1986, https://people.com/archive/enter-the-son-of-the-dragon-bruce-lees-only-boy-brandon-gets-no-kick-from-kung-fu-vol-25-no-5/.

[28] *Fort Worth Star-Telegram*, "Brandon Lee Follows Father's Footsteps," *The Baltimore Sun*, August 25, 1992, https://www.baltimoresun.com/1992/08/25/brandon-lee-follows-fathers-footsteps/.

[29] "Brandon Lee Biography," Biography.com, accessed May 3, 2024, https://www.biography.com/actors/brandon-lee.

[30] "Brandon Lee," Wikipedia, April 28, 2024, https://en.wikipedia.org/wiki/Brandon_Lee#EarlyLife.

as "Bruce Lee's only boy" but also as a "rebel without a pause." According to the *People* article, Lee was "thrown out" of two high schools for misbehavior, going on to drop out of a third.

After being kicked out at 17, he spent a few months hitchhiking across the country. He had a bit of money and would camp out in tents, working to replicate "some of the books I had read while I was growing up, *On the Road*, or whatever," he says. He would occasionally call his mom from a payphone to let her know he was okay. He eventually passed a high school equivalency test, "which [Lee] describes as 'an insult to everybody with free intelligence in the universe.'"[31]

He went on to study theater at Emerson College in Massachusetts for a year and then dropped out. Lee told *People* his time at Emerson was constraining: "Brandon didn't like Boston's Emerson College any better than high school, but he did enjoy putting on a one-man production of *Zen and the Art of Motorcycle Maintenance* during his year there." While at Emerson, he commuted to New York to study at the famous Lee Strasberg Theatre and Film Institute.

The final paragraph of the *People* article is worth quoting in full for how it encapsulates Lee's sense of humor and biting self-awareness:

> Serious acting is his goal, but for now Brandon sits in his "small, very grungy apartment" in L.A., impatiently

---

[31] "Enter the Son of the Dragon: Bruce Lee's Only Boy, Brandon, Gets No Kick from Kung Fu," *People*, February 3, 1986, https://people.com/archive/enter-the-son-of-the-dragon-bruce-lees-only-boy-brandon-gets-no-kick-from-kung-fu-vol-25-no-5/.

awaiting the results of his first break. His conversation veers from the profane to the pretentious. "I believe in the philosophy of nonconformity," says Brandon, although he is well aware of the typecasting threat his ancestry and skills create. "I don't want to be known only as Bruce Lee's son — to take a magic-carpet ride on my father's achievements. It's been very hard . . . but you could blame me too. I could have been a dentist."[32]

The "first break" the piece refers to is a supporting role in *Kung Fu: The Movie*, a 1986 made-for-TV feature follow-up to a series of the same name from the '70s starring David Carradine (a white man) as a Shaolin monk. According to Linda Lee Cadwell, Bruce developed *Kung Fu* as a vehicle for himself but lost the role to Carradine, which disappointed Bruce endlessly.[33] Lee, 21 in 1986, booked the part of Carradine's character's son while working as a script reader in L.A. and was proud to be a part of an enterprise his father had created. After *Kung Fu*, Lee's first leading role was in the 1986 Cantonese action thriller *Legacy of Rage*, a film by Ronny Yu, which wasn't released in the U.S. until 1998.

Lee returned to the small screen for a pilot called *Kung Fu: The Next Generation*, but it wasn't picked up. Between 1989 and 1992, he starred in three features: 1989's rough-hewn

---

32 Ibid.

33 Bernard Weinraub, "Bruce Lee's Brief Life Being Brought to Screen," *The New York Times*, April 15, 1993, https://www.nytimes.com/1993/04/15/movies/bruce-lee-s-brief-life-being-brought-to-screen.html.

but entertaining *Laser Mission*, 1991's buddy cop action flick *Showdown in Little Tokyo* starring Dolph Lundgren, and 1992's *Rapid Fire*. Directed by Dwight H. Little, *Rapid Fire* is a complex action thriller that allows Lee to show off his sharp comedic timing, alongside a balletic control of his body, which underscores his spellbinding martial arts skills.

*Rapid Fire*'s producer, Robert Lawrence, caught Lee in an un-dubbed screening of *Legacy of Rage* and saw Lee's potential. "The film was written for me," Lee says with well-earned pride in a *Rapid Fire* featurette.[34] In the clip, he seems proud to be working on something meaningful and grand and to finally express the whole of his creativity. He was also given the validating and emboldening opportunity to develop the fight choreography for the film along with Jeff Imada. "It's my first real, big shot, I guess," he tells Wygant with a wide grin.

Unlike Eric in *The Crow*, much of Jake's personality in *Rapid Fire* stems from Lee's personality. "I was involved with the project before there was even a script," Lee says in a 1992 interview with *The Baltimore Sun*.[35] "Not to suggest I had a lot to do with the writing," he says, reiterating what he tells Whaley. "But I did enjoy the luxury of having access to the screenwriter, Alan McElroy, while things were developing. I doubt I added much beyond just acquainting the writers with

---

34 "Introducing: Brandon Lee – The Action Hero of the 90's," YouTube, December 22, 2018, https://www.youtube.com/watch?v=IXaTzOz5HRs.

35 *Fort Worth Star-Telegram*, "Brandon Lee Follows Father's Footsteps," *The Baltimore Sun*, August 25, 1992, https://www.baltimoresun.com/1992/08/25/brandon-lee-follows-fathers-footsteps/.

the kind of personality I'd bring to the picture." Lee's Chinese American identity is crucial to the film's dynamic.

*Rapid Fire* is deeply entertaining as a tightly wound action thriller, but Lee's performance elevates it from a run-of-the-mill flick to something heady and whip-smart. Lee plays Jake Lo, an art student whose father died during the Tiananmen Square protests — Jake witnessed the incident and is consequently disillusioned with political action. The idea of sacrificing oneself for a cause is, to Jake, something that ultimately robs a family of its loved ones. Jake later witnesses a separate crime and is persuaded by a detective (played by actor Powers Boothe) to work undercover to help apprehend the perpetrators. At its core, it's a story about fathers and sons, which Lee found particularly captivating.

"Action-adventure, that genre, only works for me if you can care about the characters," Lee says in *The Baltimore Sun* interview. "If the hero's not taking some kind of a journey, then there are no stakes — and no stakes, then you don't care if he lives or dies, wins or loses," he says.[36]

The film carries Lee's understanding that a fight scene should possess the same cadence and rhythm, the same beats, as any other scene. It's a multilayered task for an actor. A fight scene, if done well, will have a character behave not only according to the personality established by the script but also in accordance with their emotional response to the narrative events that lead to the fight. Lee explains in the Whaley

---

36 Ibid.

interview that a lot of his work with "beats" was learned from Bruce, who was the first to incorporate beat-based storytelling in his fights, using dramatic, graceful, or comedic beats as the scene required. In other words, Bruce saw a fight scene as having the same nuances and depth as a dialogue-based scene. The historical importance of Bruce's work, and Brandon's after him, is similar to the importance of Gene Kelly's before them; Kelly pushed the potential of the dance number in a musical film to work alongside the narrative. Kelly's choreography (beginning with wartime musical *Cover Girl*) was one of the first on film that allowed the plot's tension to continue or be resolved or further challenged with dance; both Bruce and Brandon do the same with combat.

Lee's Jake is shown to be a sweet but arrogant young man, as many undergraduates are. At the film's beginning, he is sarcastic and world-weary, both in a literary and literal way. But as matters become dire, and as Jake's young philosophy is tested, he is prodded toward a more lenient view of things, toward a better sense of self, and toward maturation; he isn't so much turned into a fighting machine as he is allowed to learn what it looks and feels like to have something to fight for. Lee truly shines in this film — he emerges as a charismatic talent as he tempers Jake's righteous anger with warm charm and a stumbling naivete (he is often thrown into dangerous situations and trips through action, stunning himself and his combatants with his ability), delivering a complex character who learns he has a lot to learn. Gloriously shirtless and sweaty, he paints a portrait of a young man in the process of grasping the world's, the self's, and goodness's fluidity.

"I'd like to be able to show *Rapid Fire* to my dad," Lee says in the interview with *The Baltimore Sun*. "I'm that proud of what we've accomplished within the framework of the action-adventure formula." It's noteworthy that he refrains from speculating about what his father might say about the film: "No point in imagining." It becomes evident after a certain amount of research that Lee's relationship with his father was complex — perhaps more than he ever publicly let on — in the way relationships between fathers and sons often are, teetering at the intersection of expectation, responsibility, and disappointment.

In May 1993, after Lee's death on March 31 on the set of *The Crow*, the film *Dragon: The Bruce Lee Story* was released, which was based in part on Linda Lee Cadwell's book about her husband. In *Bruce Lee: the Man Only I Knew*, Cadwell traced Bruce's life, the addled perceptions of her marriage as a white woman to a Chinese man, and offered an attempt to set the record straight about Bruce's death, which is still the subject of conspiracy theories. Lee was considered by Universal Pictures for the role of his father in *Dragon*, but he turned it down, stating that the prospect frightened him and might even have been a career ender.[37, 38] He expressed a desire to

---

37 "Dragon: The Bruce Lee Story," AFI Catalog of Feature Films, accessed May 3, 2024, https://catalog.afi.com/Film/59508-DRAGON--THE-BRUCE-LEE-STORY?cxt=filmography.

38 Ryan Parker, "Brandon Lee Turned Down Role to Play His Father in 'Dragon: The Bruce Lee Story,'" *The Hollywood Reporter*, February 1, 2018, https://www.hollywoodreporter.com/movies/movie-news/brandon-lee-turned-down-role-play-his-father-dragon-bruce-lee-story-1071598/.

be perceived as a "proper" and well-rounded actor, capable in his own right, not a mere action star.[39] Lee did, however, help Jason Scott Lee, who was eventually cast as Bruce, with the role, offering some insightful advice:

> Brandon said something that was very simple. [. . .] He said I wouldn't survive in this part if I treated his father like a god. He said his father was, after all, a man who had a profound destiny, but he was not a god. He was a man who had a temper, a lot of anger, who found mediocrity offensive. Sometimes he was rather merciless.[40]

*Dragon* was released with a dedication to Brandon Lee. In 1994, a year after he passed away at the age of 28, *The Crow* was released.

## THE PRODUCTION

Brandon Lee was the first person to be cast; he came on board *The Crow* at a crucial time during the process of adapting O'Barr's story. Lee read the script before he read the comic book, but when he did read the latter, he loved it, understanding Eric as a character. Production was considering various actors

---

[39] Ibid.

[40] Bernard Weinraub, "Bruce Lee's Brief Life Being Brought to Screen," *The New York Times*, April 15, 1993, https://www.nytimes.com/1993/04/15/movies/bruce-lee-s-brief-life-being-brought-to-screen.html.

for the role, such as Christian Slater and Johnny Depp. "Then someone said, 'Did you know Bruce Lee's son is an actor?'" Proyas recalls.[41] Proyas didn't know Lee was an actor, but being a fan of Bruce, he swiftly tracked down Lee's work and found himself impressed by the young man. "When I met him, I just thought he was a really incredible person, and an amazingly charismatic guy," Proyas says. Lee and Proyas became good friends:

> He contributed script ideas and we would watch endless amounts of Hong Kong action movies together, because the action scenes in the movie were inspired by them. Particularly by John Woo's work. Brandon introduced me to a whole lot of stuff that I wasn't aware of from that world of filmmaking. It was a great creative marriage, more so than any other actor-director relationship I have had. I felt he was a storyteller along with myself, collaborating on this movie.[42]

O'Barr describes a similar sensation upon meeting Lee for the first time. O'Barr was introduced to Lee by production to see if he thought Lee would be a good fit for the part of Eric. The writer was, like Proyas, unfamiliar with Lee's work, and the night before meeting him, he watched *Rapid Fire*, which left him feeling skeptical about Lee's ability to be

---

[41] Paul Rowlands, "An Interview with Alex Proyas (Part 1 of 3)," *Money Into Light*, https://www.money-into-light.com/2017/01/an-interview-with-alex-proyas-part-1-of.html.

[42] Ibid.

frightening: "In that movie, even though he's energetic and he does the action [scenes] great, after he hit someone, he seemed almost apologetic," O'Barr says. According to him, Lee's Jake Lo had an *I didn't really mean to do that* look after he would hit an adversary, though he did appreciate Lee's undeniable screen presence. But once he met Lee, he found him a perfect match. "I couldn't picture anyone else beside[s] him after meeting him one time," O'Barr says of Lee. "He was a huge fan of the comic. He knew phrases and lines of dialog from it. He was real instrumental in keeping it faithful to the comic."

There exists somewhere on a producer's shelf a 90-minute on-set interview conducted with Lee while he is in full Eric Draven costume. According to O'Barr, in the '90s, the producers decided against releasing the interview in its entirety. "It's where he's talking about all the action scenes and the gunplay," O'Barr says.[43] A five-minute and 41-second clip excerpted from the longer interview is available on YouTube, and in it, Lee describes wearing squibs (blood packs that explode to imitate bleeding after a bullet wound). "I just got shot 20 times," Lee says with a wide grin on his face.[44] "[Producers] were like, 'We don't want anyone to see that since he got shot,'" O'Barr recalls with disdain. "[The interviews] are great because [Lee] says a lot of really philosophical

---

43 Philip Anderson, "Interviews: James O'Barr - Author of The Crow," *KAOS2000 Magazine*, July 20, 2000, archived March 23, 2016, https://web.archive.org/web/20160323220745/http://kaos2000.net/interviews/jamesobarr/.

44 "The Crow Brandon Lee on Set Interview Rare 1993," YouTube, November 13, 2022, https://www.youtube.com/watch?v=ke75Cab4I70&t=207s.

elements throughout the thing. It's stupid. They don't think, 'We'll never see another film from this guy' because he's gone. It's just sitting on the shelf somewhere. It's aggravating to me."[45]

The short clip is electrifying. In it, Lee sits with his long black hair shrouding his painted face, smoking a cigarette. He seems mellow here — it's unclear whether he's trying to stay in character or is tired, or both — his head bent low, he looks up desultorily between his locks, affectively brooding like Eric Draven. However, he can't help himself, and his bright personality and sarcasm bubble to the surface as he playfully answers the interviewer's questions, prefacing his straight answers with saucy quips. He sits so still that his cigarette smoke hangs about his face, lacing through his hair like a cloud; it's tough to see his face except when he smiles, at which point his black-painted lips open wide and his brilliant teeth shine through. Even though he says that particular day is a "no acting required day," it makes sense that he would stay in character because, for Lee, how a character moves and reacts to his environment needs to be informed by who they are essentially; how he jerks and falls when hit by a rainfall of bullets needs to be in line with Eric Draven's psychology.

---

[45] Philip Anderson, "Interviews: James O'Barr - Author of The Crow," *KAOS2000 Magazine*, July 20, 2000, archived March 23, 2016, https://web.archive.org/web/20160323220745/http://kaos2000.net/interviews/jamesobarr/.

The film is truly faithful to the graphic novel, maintaining all of its grimy and seedy essence, its subversive and countercultural ethos. Certain small details stray from O'Barr's version. Eric becomes Eric Draven, and Shelly, played by Sofia Shinas, gets the last name Webster. The two live in a tenement in Detroit. Eric, a mechanic in the comic, becomes here a rock musician (in homage to the importance of music in O'Barr's original) in a grunge band called Hangman's Joke.

A goon named Top Dollar (Michael Wincott) controls much of the city. When Shelly submits a petition to the city against proposed evictions — intended to simply empty the building so it might be burned on Devil's Night — she is really giving Top Dollar the middle finger. On Devil's Night, October 30, Top Dollar sends his minions — T-Bird (David Patrick Kelly), Skank (Angel David), Tin Tin (Laurence Mason), and Fun Boy (Michael Massee) — to the couple's apartment, tasked with the mission of persuading Shelly to rescind her petition. The gang attacks and rapes her. Eric interrupts them, and the mission turns to murder as the gang shoots him and flings him out of the sixth-story window. Officer Albrecht (Ernie Hudson) is first on the scene of the crime and is heartbroken by Eric and Shelly's tragic love story.

The young girl, who appears as Sherri, in the book becomes Sarah (played by Rochelle Davis) in the film. Her friendships with Eric and Shelly and with Albrecht were fleshed out further after Lee's death to fill in any remaining narrative gaps.[46] The gaps were originally meant to contain a character called Skull Cowboy (played by Michael Berryman), who would explain the rules of the afterlife to Eric. The Skull Cowboy character does appear a handful of times in O'Barr's book — as a sort of Grim Reaper or image of death — but he is not an expository character in the way The Crow is. Lee's scenes with Berryman hadn't been completed before his passing, so the Skull Cowboy was removed, with Sarah's narration added to the film's beginning.

The body of the film, the "present," is as monochromatic as was allowed. Proyas wanted to film in black and white because, after all, the comic book is in black and white, alive with O'Barr's charged ink, but was barred by the producers. Proyas's workaround was to use filters and practical optical effects to wash out any bright colors, reserving a sort of warm orange-red, a bit like marigolds, for Eric's memories of Shelly. The present is hard and wet, with rain and steam used to blur and dull brightness, to make it seem as though it's always behind a sheen of tears, as if we're looking through Eric's perennial wet eyes. The present is unfriendly and tough and bleak, while the past becomes warm as a bed, soft as a promise of eternal love.

Lee, too, wanted the film to be in black and white to stay as faithful to the source material as possible. "I would have deeply loved to shoot the whole film in black and white. Personally,

---

46 Rebecca Ascher-Walsh, "How *The Crow* Flew," *Entertainment Weekly*, May 13, 1994, archived March 14, 2022, https://archive.org/details/entertainment-weekly-222-1994-05-13-brandon-lee-his-last-interview/page/18/mode/1up?view=theater.

I love black and white. I think it's wonderful," Lee says with a frank smile on the featurette. "It would have been great to do that and show perhaps just the flashbacks, which are a part of Eric's real life, his life when he was alive, show those in color, as contrast. But, unfortunately, due to the realities, the very shitty realities of the film world, we weren't given the opportunity to do that."

There is a sense, in the film's featurette, that the producers don't fully understand the film as viscerally as Proyas and Lee do. Co-producer Jeff Most calls Eric an "everyman," unremarkable in life but remarkable in death. But Lee understands that Eric was never an everyman, understands that a love so powerful as to transcend death isn't a mundane thing. This is why, after all, Eric's memories of bliss become daggers that haunt him like unrelenting shadows, looming menacingly until they consume him and carry him along in their undertow.

From the few interviews with Lee that exist, it is abundantly evident that he thought very deeply about O'Barr's story, crawled into Eric as a character, and understood his inner workings. This worming-in is unsurprising; after all, Lee trained at the Lee Strasberg Institute, which pioneered method acting. According to the method, an actor should think, *What in me — my past, my personality, my essence — would make me perform like this character?*

In considering Lee's words about Eric, it is evident he was putting the method to work. The featurette's interview, conducted by Ira Teller, is the one that *Entertainment Weekly* refers to as Lee's "last interview." The print article contains lines from the interview that don't appear in the short video, such as Lee offering insight into how he tackled Eric as a project. For example, he offers an image that has allowed him to understand the weight life holds for Eric after his death. It's an image that has now become inextricably tied to Brandon Lee; it's a quotation from Paul Bowles's 1949 novel *The Sheltering Sky*, which marks Lee's grave.

He recites the quotation as easily and effortlessly as one might put on shoes before heading out the door.

> Because we do not know when we will die, we get to think of life as an inexhaustible well, and yet everything happens only a certain number of times and a very small number, really. How many more times will you remember a certain afternoon of your childhood, an afternoon . . . that is so deeply a part of your being you can't even conceive of your life without it? Perhaps four or five times more? Perhaps not even that. How many more times will you watch the full moon rise? Perhaps, twenty. And yet it all seems limitless.[47]

He seems to have a fiery philosophical bent in his curiosity, the kind in all the best actors. Lee, remaining earnest as he ever was, even in his self-awareness, goes on to explain what

---

[47] Ira Teller, "Brandon Lee's Last Interview," *Entertainment Weekly*, May 13, 1994, archived March 14, 2022, https://archive.org/details/entertainment-weekly-222-1994-05-13-brandon-lee-his-last-interview/page/22/mode/1up?view=theater.

this long quotation, delivered with the gravitas and reverence worthy of a John Milton verse, means. Because we often don't think about our death, we tend to think we're going to live forever, and so we take a lot for granted. But when we come face to face with death, we realize the importance of many things. Eric utters a much shorter and punchier iteration of this in the film, saying, "Nothing is trivial."

Armed with an understanding of himself, with reference to Bowles, Lee put himself in Eric's shoes and considered what would be most important to him if he were to die and be brought back to life. "[W]ho would I want to see? The person would be my fiancée, Eliza [Hutton], because I'm getting married after the film. And the thing about Eric is, the one person he would want to share this with isn't there anymore. And that's the tragic element of this character," Lee tells Teller. Lee understood what it was within him that would prompt him to act like Eric Draven, he understood the color and flavor and texture of Eric's loss, and because of this understanding, he played Eric's grief with a preternaturally resonant gusto.

So much of Lee's commitment seems to stem from a genuine curiosity for not only Eric Draven but the act of filmmaking itself, what it means to be an actor, to do one's job with intelligence and responsibility. He goes on to say that the film's violence is justified because if he were in Eric's position, he would burn everything down, too.

✳

Lee's espousal of the method wasn't reckless or deleterious to others, toxic in the way that has made the technique infamous in recent years. Jared Leto staying in character as the Joker and sending live and dead animals to his cast members comes immediately to mind. And Christian Bale, who unhealthily lost weight in a short period of time for *The Machinist*, subsisting on a diet of cigarettes and apples so he could look skeletal. In the few on-set and behind-the-scenes clips I have seen, Lee seems in very good spirits, professional in front of the camera, and jovial when not, laughing with cast members and joking with crew. He seems to be having a blast, even as he is putting in the work to make a good thing of *The Crow*.

In Ascher-Walsh's piece for *Entertainment Weekly* that corrals cast and crew members' feelings after Lee's passing, so many remark upon Lee's friendliness on set. Lance Anderson did Lee's makeup and became very close with the actor, relating to him as a father would his son — Anderson's own son was the same age as Lee at the time. Anderson sweetly notes needing to rein it in when doing Lee's makeup: "I had to keep low-key, because if I started talking, it would set Brandon off on a story, and we would be in for an extra half hour of makeup. He loved Game Boy — he was addicted to it. I'd be painting these delicate lines on his face, and he'd hit a point on the game, and it would be time for a cleanup job."[48]

---

[48] Rebecca Ascher-Walsh, "How *The Crow* Flew," *Entertainment Weekly*, May 13, 1994, archived March 14, 2022, https://archive.org/details/entertainment-weekly-222-1994-05-13-brandon-lee-his-last-interview/page/18/mode/1up?view=theater.

Still photographer for the film Robert Zuckerman recalls Lee's charm and his passion for the project: "He had a boyish enthusiasm, but he was very focused... He would always go the extra mile. We could be at the end of a long day, with a lot of rain machines going, and everyone would be happy with the shot. He could have gone [home] and chilled out, but Brandon would cock his head and call out to Alex, 'What if we did it this way?'"[49]

In the interview with Teller, Lee is frank when asked about the physical toll filming has had on him. Teller brings up the idea of destiny, its importance in the film, and goes on to ask Lee about his own destiny. "Oh, now we're gonna talk about me, huh?" Lee says, and it's not too tough to imagine him smiling that big, warm smile of his. "Well, I'm freezing to death; it's so cold in here! Was I destined to play this role? I don't know if I was destined to play this role, but I feel very fortunate to be doing so."

Filming took place in Wilmington, North Carolina, in the dead of winter amongst miniatures that Proyas had built especially for the film — a dark and damned city with black in its cobbled veins. It was cold, so cold that the actors' breaths are sometimes perceptible in the film, little clouds escaping their mouths as if carrying the ghosts of their words. In the final scene, Lee's Eric is veritably steaming in the cold, the heat rising off his body in wisps. "When he filmed the sequence coming out of the grave, [it] was 5 degrees," recalls O'Barr in Ascher-Walsh's article. "They had to put alcohol in the rain

---

49 Ibid.

machines to keep the liquid from freezing, and all Brandon had on were his pants. But he did the scene over and over until he got it exactly as he wanted it. He was a hell of a trouper."

Much of the filming was done at night under heavy artificial rainfall. "I've been colder on this film than I've been in years," Lee told Teller. "I can never remember deliberately going outside when it was about 5 degrees, in the rain, with no shoes on," he says, referring to the film's opening. But he notes that the discomfort is, to an extent, justified by the story. "It's extreme," he says. "The character comes back from the dead, and, at first he doesn't know where he is, how he got there ... How does that tie in with the physicality? I just don't think he should be too healthy-looking, so I lost some weight for the role. [...] I think it adds to the character's experience," he says of the cold and toll on his body. "I mean, he's torn up emotionally, physically, and psychically, and the fact that there have been some stringent physical demands placed on me [has] only been helpful in creating the environment."

"He was one of the nicest people," said Rochelle Davis, 13 years old at the time. "The only thing I didn't like about him was he didn't like dogs. He hated them because he said they always bit him."[50]

Filming from the start was troubled, hounded by so many mishaps; many on the crew felt as though production was cursed. Not only did filming persist during a blizzard and withstand a hurricane that tore through the set, destroying

---

50 Ibid.

much of it, there were also a number of accidents. On the first day of filming, a carpenter sustained serious burns on his torso. Later, a screwdriver went through a worker's hand, a truck full of equipment caught fire, a stuntperson fell through a roof and broke his ribs, and a set sculptor drove his car through a props room (whether accidentally or intentionally, it is unclear).[51] (I read a fact once that I've not been able to find again to corroborate that said that drug use, specifically of cocaine, was so rampant on set among crew members that when a person once sneezed, Lee said, "Someone just lost $50.")

And then there was what happened to Lee. The accident took place early morning on March 31, 1993. Lee was nearing the end of his days on set, with only three remaining on his schedule. His wedding to Hutton was scheduled for April 17, 1993; it was the glowing beacon on his horizon. "The night prior to the accident I asked him what he was working on next," remembered Shinas. "He said, 'Getting married.'" They were filming the earliest scene when Eric walks in on Shelly being attacked. Michael Massee, as Fun Boy, shot Eric according to script, but when Lee fell, it was not in the proper manner. Jeff Imada checked Lee after Proyas called "cut" and found him unconscious and breathing heavily. Lee was rushed to hospital after the on-site medic checked him, noticing after a few minutes a dire irregularity in his heartbeat. Lee underwent six hours of surgery, never regaining consciousness and passing away at 1:03 p.m. on March 31.

---

51 "The Crow," IMDb, accessed May 3, 2024, https://www.imdb.com/title/tt0109506/trivia/?item=tr2585918&ref_=ext_shr_lnk.

The gun Massee fired at Lee was a real revolver loaded with blank rounds. A blank round is just the cartridge component accompanied by gunpowder and primer but no actual bullet. When loaded into a firearm and fired, a blank round creates the sound and flash a real gunshot makes because it contains a real gunpowder charge, but because it does not have the projectile bullet in it, nothing actually hits the target.[52] Blanks are used easily in prop guns, but a real firearm would need to be modified to fire a blank. During the filming of an earlier close-up scene that used the same revolver, hollowed-out dummy rounds (the projectile bullet part) were placed into the gun to make it appear as though it was really loaded.[53] Dummy rounds don't contain propellant or gunpowder and, therefore, can't be shot.

It was a dummy bullet from this earlier close-up scene that became lodged in the gun's barrel, unbeknownst to the actors and crew. In an interview O'Barr gave in 2000, he hinted that non-union workers had handled the gun the night before, accidentally leaving behind the lodged dummy bullet.[54] A gun loaded with a blank round and a dummy round will combine the bullet with the charge; the blank creates a flash and a bang because of the gunpowder, which then propels the dummy

---

[52] Giulia Heyward, "Actor Brandon Lee Was Killed by a Prop Gun, Years Before the 'Rust' Shooting Death," NPR, January 20, 2023, https://www.npr.org/2023/01/20/1150034900/brandon-lee-killed-prop-gun-rust-shooting-death-alec-baldwin-halyna-hutchins.

[53] "No Charges Filed in Actor's Death During Filming," *The New York Times*, September 6, 1993, https://www.nytimes.com/1993/09/06/us/no-charges-filed-in-actor-s-death-during-filming.html.

[54] Philip Anderson, "Interviews: James O'Barr - Author of The Crow," *KAOS2000 Magazine*, July 20, 2000, archived March 23, 2016, https://web.archive.org/web/20160323220745/http:/kaos2000.net/interviews/jamesobarr/.

toward whatever the barrel is aimed at. Such a gun would fire much like a real gun with a live round.

According to *The New York Times*, reporting in 1993, "[t]he cartridge popped during filming [the close-up] and lodged the bullet in the top of the gun barrel until it was dislodged when the blank was fired. The gun was not inspected between the filming of that scene and the scene shot early in the morning of March 31."[55] The dummy rounds were poorly made by crew members, who had run out of actual dummy bullets and, to save time, fashioned their own out of live rounds by removing the gunpowder; they should have waited a day to buy legitimate dummy bullets from a licensed firearms dealer.[56] The night before / early morning of Lee's death, the arms specialist had been sent home, and the person working the props wasn't aware of handling protocol — the gun should have been checked and cleared before the blank was fired. It struck Lee in the abdomen from less than 20 feet away; Lee was not wearing a bulletproof vest.[57] The shot created "an entry wound approximately the size of a silver dollar."[58]

---

55 "No Charges Filed in Actor's Death During Filming," *The New York Times*, September 6, 1993, https://www.nytimes.com/1993/09/06/us/no-charges-filed-in-actor-s-death-during-filming.html.

56 Terry Pristin, "Brandon Lee's Mother Claims Negligence Caused His Death : Movies: Linda Lee Cadwell Sues 14 Entities Regarding the Actor's 'Agonizing Pain, Suffering and Untimely Death' Last March on the North Carolina Set of 'The Crow,'" *Los Angeles Times*, August 11, 1993, https://www.latimes.com/archives/la-xpm-1993-08-11-ca-22553-story.html.

57 "Brandon Lee," Wikipedia, April 28, 2024, https://en.wikipedia.org/wiki/Brandon_Lee#Death.

58 Terry Pristin, "Brandon Lee's Mother Claims Negligence Caused His Death : Movies: Linda Lee Cadwell Sues 14 Entities Regarding the Actor's 'Agonizing Pain, Suffering and Untimely Death' Last March on the North Carolina Set of 'The Crow.'," *Los Angeles Times*, August 11, 1993, https://www.latimes.com/archives/la-xpm-1993-08-11-ca-22553-story.html.

Interviewed by Ascher-Walsh, Shinas was distraught when the cast and crew were called back to North Carolina to complete production. She was on the soundstage and witnessed the accident. "I was an emotional wreck," she said. Shinas explained that the only reason she went back to Wilmington was because she was contractually obligated. "It was never technically [questioned] if we could complete it — it was always evident that Brandon's role was basically done," said producer Pressman. Jeff Most echoed a similarly cold and business-minded tone: "The issue was psychological," Most said. "It was only through Eliza's great dedication to Brandon that we pushed on . . . She knew how important this was to him, and that it would have been his wish to complete it." Ascher-Walsh follows the producers' unsympathetic words with a quote from an unnamed source, who said, "All she did was agree to have them complete the film [. . .] Instinctively, she would have preferred not to deal with it at all."

Back on set, the crew and cast moved "slowly," according to Lance Anderson, deliberately taking their time so as not to rush or hurry and make a mistake. "There was a calmness on the set that hadn't been there before [and] plenty of time to get everything done correctly," the makeup artist said.

Production had begun in February 1993 and was intended to end after 54 days; it was cut a few days short of the target on March 31. Pressman asked cast and crew to come back to the set six weeks later, on May 26, to finish the film. *The Crow* officially completed production on June 28, 1993, the day I was born, curiously. What was left un-filmed were scenes meant to further flesh out Eric and Shelly's relationship — in the final cut, memories of the past appear as montages without much dialogue, but they were intended to strike a register closer to the hazy and lingering vignettes depicted in the comic.

Eventually, Lee's death was ruled an accident after an investigation. District Attorney Jerry Spivey declared that "there was no evidence of wrongdoing."[59] Spivey said that a part of him wanted to file charges against Crowvision, the production company behind *The Crow*. Spivey was looking into state laws around holding corporations criminally liable but, eventually, couldn't pursue such a charge. Spivey noted that there was negligence leading up to Lee's death, but "[t]here is no evidence pointing to the kind of negligence the criminal law seeks to punish," he said.[60] Lee's mother, Linda Lee Cadwell, did file a civil lawsuit against the filmmakers (Crowvision Inc. and the Edward R. Pressman Film Corp.) and settled for an undisclosed sum.[61]

Massee was hit hard. In a rare interview with *Extra* in 2005, he said he "wasn't even supposed to be handling the gun in the scene until we started shooting the scene and the director changed it." Massee took a year off from acting and went to New York, where he wasn't emotionally ready to work. "What happened to Brandon was a tragic accident. I

---

59 "No Charges Filed in Actor's Death During Filming," *The New York Times*, September 6, 1993, https://www.nytimes.com/1993/09/06/us/no-charges-filed-in-actor-s-death-during-filming.html.

60 Ibid.

61 Shauna Snow, "Legal File: Brandon Lee Case Settled: Linda Lee...," *Los Angeles Times*, October 27, 1993, https://www.latimes.com/archives/la-xpm-1993-10-27-ca-50050-story.html.

don't think you ever get over something like that," he said.[62] "It's something I'm going to live with. It took me the time it took to be able to not so much put it in perspective but to be able to move on with my life. [. . .] It's very personal. It's something that I wanna make sure when I work that it's never repeated. Therefore, I'm very conscious of things going awry on set."[63] He passed away in 2016.

Proyas was a wreck as he faced the obstacle of putting the film together after the loss of a person who had become a dear friend. "Honestly, I have no idea what that movie is," the director said in 2016. "I haven't seen it since we finished it." He said the only reason he went back to work on it was because Lee's family wanted it that way. "Throughout the whole process, I was pretty much in a haze. I had lost a really good friend. That to me was the most difficult part of the process. All I could do was to stick to the plan that was conceived originally. I was in no fit state to redesign the wheel. I can't actually say much about the film aesthetically in any way because I just don't remember it very well. I've pretty much put it from my mind because of the pain from the experience that happened."[64]

Lee's sister Shannon, who was 24 at the time, recalls being shattered after the event, falling into a deep depression. She

---

62 "Michael Massee on Extra: Talks About Brandon Lee Shooting," YouTube, April 2, 2007, https://www.youtube.com/watch?v=Zjn3WqsvE_Q.

63 Toyin Owoseje, "Brandon Lee's Family Speak Out After Fatal Prop Gun Shooting on Set," CNN, October 22, 2021, https://www.cnn.com/2021/10/22/entertainment/brandon-lee-family-speaks-out-halyna-hutchins-death-intl-scli/index.html.

64 Paul Rowlands, "An Interview with Alex Proyas (Part 1 of 3)," *Money Into Light*, 2016, https://www.money-into-light.com/2017/01/an-interview-with-alex-proyas-part-1-of.html.

flew to Wilmington from her home in New Orleans as soon as she heard about the shooting. During the flight, she had the overwhelming feeling that Brandon had passed away, even though there was no way for anyone to contact her mid-flight. She and Lee had planned for the future. She was to serve as best woman at his wedding, and she was planning on moving to L.A. to pursue acting and be closer to her brother. She fell upon her father's notebooks, reading them for the first time, and found advice similar to O'Barr's note on forgiveness: "The medicine for my suffering I had within me from the very beginning, but I didn't take it." She said in an interview, "It just hit me in the chest. It told me: the only person who can solve this for you is you."[65]

Since Lee's death, Shannon has been staunch in her support of banning live guns from film sets, and after cinematographer Halyna Hutchins was killed by a live round in a prop gun in 2021, she expressed her condolences through Brandon Lee's tribute X page, which she runs: "No one should ever be killed by a gun on a film set," she wrote. "Period."[66]

Shannon, who worked as Lee's assistant on *Rapid Fire*, remembers her brother as "a big, boisterous ball of energy" who was her "tormentor" in the best way: he loved to play pranks on

---

[65] Ann Lee, "Life Without Bruce and Brandon: Shannon Lee on Losing Her Superstar Father and Brother," *The Guardian*, April 15, 2024, https://www.theguardian.com/film/2024/apr/15/life-without-bruce-and-brandon-shannon-lee-on-losing-her-superstar-father-and-brother.

[66] Brandon Bruce Lee (@brandonlee), "Our hearts go out to the family of Halyna Hutchins and to Joel Souza and all involved in the incident on 'Rust'. No one should ever be killed by a gun on a film set. Period. 💔," Twitter (now X), October 22, 2021, https://twitter.com/brandonblee/status/1451401745419030531.

her. "But when it mattered, he was also my protector," she says. "If someone was being mean to me, he would step in."[67]

After news of Hutchins's death broke, Eliza Hutton posted a photo of her and Lee to Instagram on October 26, 2021. It appears at the beginning of *The Crow*, standing in as a picture of Eric and Shelly, which Eric looks at and then later burns. Hutton's back is draped in a lace and satin wedding dress that she is trying on, and Lee embraces her while facing a mirror. He's smiling as he snaps the photo of the two of them. "There is no such thing as a prop gun," Hutton captioned the photo.[68] The next day, she posted a photo of Lee. "Failing to follow gun safety protocol on a movie set is not an 'accident,'" she wrote, "it is negligence. Please educate and protect yourself."[69] Her words are few and dry but incendiary and indemnifying.

O'Barr and Hutton became close after Lee's death. She helped him deal with his compounded survivor's guilt. "It's actually like Brandon's death brought things full circle for me," O'Barr said in a 2000 interview.[70] "It gave me the perspective that I couldn't find before. So something good did

---

67 Ann Lee, "Life Without Bruce and Brandon: Shannon Lee on Losing Her Superstar Father and Brother," *The Guardian*, April 15, 2024, https://www.theguardian.com/film/2024/apr/15/life-without-bruce-and-brandon-shannon-lee-on-losing-her-superstar-father-and-brother.

68 Eliza Hutton (@fotosbyeliza), "There is no such thing as a prop gun. #brandonlee," Instagram, October 26, 2021, https://www.instagram.com/fotosbyeliza/p/CVerWOlFaqp/.

69 Eliza Hutton (@fotosbyeliza), "Failing to follow gun safety protocol on a movie set is not an 'accident,' it is negligence. Please educate and protect yourself. #brandonlee," Instagram, October 27, 2021, https://www.instagram.com/fotosbyeliza/p/CVi-dh6BDfq/.

70 Philip Anderson, "Interviews: James O'Barr - Author of The Crow," *KAOS2000 Magazine*, July 20, 2000, archived March 23, 2016, https://web.archive.org/web/20160323220745/http://kaos2000.net/interviews/jamesobarr/.

come out of it for me, at least." O'Barr thanks Hutton in the acknowledgment section of his book's 2010 special edition "for her compassion and friendship." And he also thanks Proyas and Lee "for taking my scribbles and putting breath and blood and bone to them on the big screen." Here and in interviews, O'Barr's love is abundantly evident for Proyas and especially Lee, the true creative forces behind the film.

It's curious, but in a panel not accompanied by any words — part of a handful of images O'Barr added to the end of the special edition — it seems as though he's added Lee and Hutton into a carousel of Eric and Shelly, kissing, embracing, and laughing. The blonde Shelly becomes brunette like Hutton for a mesmerizing flash as she holds Eric/Lee close and kisses him. His eyes are open as though he is watching in disbelief at having found such a resounding and eternal love. The panel's resemblance to a photo Hutton posted on her Instagram for Lee's birthday in 2023 is uncanny. Her honeyed hair is piled loosely atop her head, and she and Lee are kissing, just like in O'Barr's panel, which seems a sweet memorial to Lee and Hutton's love that, like Eric and Shelly's, burned bright and beautifully and powerfully, if only for a moment in time.

"Remember when you said 'Mine' and I said 'Forever.' You said 'Only forever?' *It's forever, now*," Eric says in the graphic novel, his final words.

## RECEPTION THEN

After Lee's death and what Jeff Most called the ensuing "difficult press coverage," after the cast and crew took some time off, Paramount withdrew its support.[71] Miramax Films stepped in, adding $8 million to the budget to facilitate the film's completion. They went on, of course, to make a lot of money in return, so much so that one wonders if news of Lee's death impacted the film's success. It was the highest-grossing film its first weekend and was the biggest opener for Miramax up until that point in 1994.[72] The film, buttressed by an extensive advertising campaign on TV which heavily featured the film's stacked soundtrack, had a big opening across 1,573 screens, Miramax's then widest release; it would go on to reel in $93.7 million against its $23 million budget.[73, 74]

The film's later expansion to 1,900 screens indicates Miramax's confidence that it would continue to do well, but, curiously, according to the *Los Angeles Times*, "box-office receipts on Saturday night, traditionally the week's biggest — were off the pace of Friday's opening night, according to some exhibition

---

[71] Rebecca Ascher-Walsh, "How *The Crow* Flew," *Entertainment Weekly*, May 13, 1994, archived March 14, 2022, https://archive.org/details/entertainment-weekly-222-1994-05-13-brandon-lee-his-last-interview/page/18/mode/1up?view=theater.

[72] David J Fox, "'The Crow' Takes Off at Box Office : Movies: The Opening Is the Biggest Ever for Miramax. In Second Place Is 'When a Man Loves a Woman,' with 'Crooklyn' Third," *Los Angeles Times*, May 16, 1994, https://www.latimes.com/archives/la-xpm-1994-05-16-ca-58401-story.html.

[73] Ibid.

[74] Umberto Gonzalez, "'The Crow': Everything We Know About the Reimagining So Far," *The Wrap*, March 15, 2024, https://www.thewrap.com/the-crow-remake-everything-we-know/.

sources. Situations like that are not the typical pattern for movies that have healthy runs of many consecutive weeks." Nonetheless, the film was a relative success. The *Los Angeles Times* noted that "Lee's popularity is somewhat akin to that of James Dean, the actor who died in a car crash with two just-completed films, 'Rebel Without a Cause' and 'Giant,' still to come out."[75]

Roger Ebert enjoyed *The Crow*, giving it three and a half stars out of five in a very tender review. Noting the layers of irony that cake the film — a young man brought to life in the way Lee is through the film — his review goes on to praise the film for its miniatures and practical and special effects. But Ebert's review overwhelmingly praises Lee, stating not only that the film is more of a screen achievement than any of Bruce Lee's films but also that in the face of earlier talks about shelving it, he is ultimately glad that the film was released. "At least what Brandon Lee accomplished — in a film that looks to have been hard, dedicated labor — has been preserved." Ebert's words concede that Lee's death casts a sharp and distinct shadow over the picture: "the fact of his death cannot help providing a melancholy subtext to everything he does on screen, and to all of his speeches about death and revenge."[76]

Film critic James Berardinelli's review echoes Ebert's sentiment, stating in 1994 that the irony will be lost on few. His

---

[75] David J. Fox, "'The Crow' Takes Off at Box Office : Movies: The Opening Is the Biggest Ever for Miramax. In Second Place Is 'When a Man Loves a Woman,' with 'Crooklyn' Third," *Los Angeles Times*, May 16, 1994, https://www.latimes.com/archives/la-xpm-1994-05-16-ca-58401-story.html.

[76] Roger Ebert, "Reviews: The Crow," movie review and film summary, RogerEbert.com, May 13, 1994, https://www.rogerebert.com/reviews/the-crow-1994.

use of words, though, is a bit strange (more on this later) as he calls the matter of Lee's death "a case of 'art imitating death,'" perhaps failing to recall that the statement doesn't make sense in the timeline of the film's production. Berardinelli's review does state that Lee's death will always hang over the film as a specter, but Proyas's adept direction elevates the film above its sad history, saying that it's a "fitting epitaph" for Lee.[77]

Critic Desson Howe's review for *The Washington Post*, also notes the irony and says that the film is haunted by Lee, haunted in every frame. In what is an overwhelmingly negative review, Howe says that the film is elevated *because* of the accident: "An otherwise respectable pop noir is transformed into something eerie and deeply compelling."[78] It's a horrifying statement to make, to intimate that were it not for the accident, the film would be quite run-of-the-mill. In the review, Howe calls the story corny and all the characters simple and archetypal, with their dialogue "a collection of cartoon-balloon hokum." It's a sarcastic mess of a review that argues "irony" is what saves the film. Even as Howe's review says that the film is "too stylized to take seriously," it maintains that Proyas has "composed the perfect swan song," which would be a strange thing to claim if one recalls that this is Proyas's debut. But, unsurprisingly, again, Howe's review is terribly, insensitively talking about Lee: "If he had to die so soon, this movie is the best and most appropriate send-off Lee could

---

[77] James Berardinelli, "Review: The Crow," *Reelviews*, 1994, https://preview.reelviews.net/movies/c/crow.html.

[78] Desson Howe, "'The Crow' (R)," *The Washington Post*, May 13, 1994, https://www.washingtonpost.com/wp-srv/style/longterm/movies/videos/thecrowrhowe_a0b055.htm.

have hoped for." As Howe's review paints a strange ouroboros — according to his logic, the film is the best "send-off" Lee could hope for, but only because Lee's death makes it the "best and most appropriate send-off" — he reveals the pitfalls of couching criticism in facile (not to mention cold) perceptions of irony.

A much kinder review in *Variety* calls the film seamless and pulsating, "one of the most effective live-actioners ever derived from a comic strip."[79] This review, too, notes a simplistic script and uninvolved dialogue, along with a lack of twists and turns, but that is helped along, or lifted from obscurity, by enticing set design, soundtrack, and intrigue about Lee's death, which give the film "very strong commercial wings." The review uses the word "irony" only once. *Variety* states that Lee's "striking looks, sinuous presence and agile moves lock one's attention, and the painful irony of his role as a dead man returning from the grave will not go unnoticed."

It had its more committed detractors, too, who didn't like the film in its own right. "The film is haunted by a reworked script that may be weighed down by Lee's memory, making it a bit of a morality play and a little faux sentimental," Anderson Jones, critic for the *Detroit Free Press*, wrote in 1994.[80]

Time and again, it is said the film resembles a long music video. Some fault the film for this, while others praise it, as in Ebert's case: "At times the film looks like a violent music video,

---

[79] Todd McCarthy, "Reviews: The Crow," *Variety*, April 29, 1994, https://variety.com/1994/film/reviews/the-crow-1200436537/.

[80] Anderson Jones, "'Crow' Eerily Parallels Brandon Lee's Real Life," *Detroit Free Press*, archived April 26, 2002, https://www.newspapers.com/article/detroit-free-press-the-crow/100530222/.

all image and action, no content. If it had developed more story and characterization, however, it might not have had quite the same success in evoking a world where the bizarre reality, not the story, is the point." In other words, according to Ebert, the film offers something unique or edgy, something special because it compellingly depicts a cruel and frightful world, thanks to Proyas's visual aesthetic and cinematographer Dariusz Wolski's auric moodiness. Had it offered the characterization or fleshing out that other reviewers crave, the film might have lost its unique angle and become heavy-handed for mixing such a distinct aesthetic with literary characterization.

In the same year, journalist Arlene R. Weiss conducted an interview with James O'Barr that wasn't published until 2011. She wrote:

> In May 1994, a popular cultural phenomenon swept the nation when the motion picture adaptation of *The Crow* was released. A brilliant and starkly vivid visual realization of the adult underground cult graphic novel by author and illustrator James O'Barr, it *became something of an instant legend due to the tragedy* of it being the final performance of the truly gifted and eloquent actor, Brandon Lee (son of martial arts actor and legend Bruce Lee). Lee was accidentally killed by a malfunctioning prop gun on the film's set during the making of the film. *[Italics mine.]*[81]

---

[81] Arlene R. Weiss, "Interview with 'The Crow' Author, Artist, Musician James O'Barr: 'Let the Picture Tell the Story,'" *Guitar International*, September 26, 2011, archived November 14, 2011, https://web.archive.org/web/20111114095911/http:/guitarinternational.com/2011/10/04/interview-with-the-crow-author-artist-musician-james-obarr-let-the-picture-tell-the-story/.

This belief that the film is a cult darling *because* of its real-life tragedy is certainly easy and quick, and maybe it is true, maybe some people did head to the theaters in 1994 because of what they saw in the news. The word "irony" is appealing for how it neatly papers over something more complex: the conjunction and frisson of the film's literal and narrative tragedies with its emotional power.

Across these reviews, though, it can be seen that *something* about *The Crow* stuck to these reviewers, a *something* that they were only able to vocalize clumsily in their terse praise for Lee, or vaguely and lazily, as the irony of it all. So much of the core dynamic of these reviews, their theses, hinges on the literal fact of Lee's death and its interaction with the plot, with the term "irony" used as a creative shorthand in a way that seems anachronistic to me, or something like a logical fallacy. To be fair, Lee's death was, after all, a fresh cultural wound, a tragedy so recent that seeing the film in all its literal and visceral complexity perhaps is only possible with some time and distance.

INTERPRETATION NOW

To this day, when people talk about *The Crow*, they bring up the irony. Soon after I became obsessed with *The Crow*, a critic friend asked me, with genuine curiosity, if I was so enthralled with the film *because* of Lee's death. I've been told many times (by men, specifically and curiously) that the acting is hammy. These folks believe this tragedy is the reason why the film is a cult favorite, why sentimental audiences take a liking to the film despite its "obvious" badness; they believe that the scandal and its potential for romanticization is why so many return to the film. When I showed the film to The Boy I Was Trying to Forget during one of the final times I saw him, he, an actor himself, refused to give the film a rating higher than 7 out of 10. He acknowledged the strength of Lee's performance, but he couldn't say the film was holistically great, finding it subpar and nothing to write home about.

Did the tragedy, a kind of sentimentality or romanticism, yoke me to the film? The truthful answer is that it wasn't the tragedy at all (I didn't even learn much about Lee's death onset until after my first watch of the film). It was its core, where I saw something alive and aching, like a beating heart beneath the floorboards.

When I was researching this book, I read through a post on Reddit that exclaims jubilantly, as though the poster were the first to consider the film apart from Lee's accident, "*The Crow* is bad. Really bad."[82] The post then goes on to delineate all the ways in which the film is bad, effectively faulting the film for what Ebert et al. also faulted it for: insufficient character exposition, telling instead of showing, a contrived ending that is "hilariously bad." They say the film is boring, that there are no stakes, ultimately stating that "[t]here is nothing to the story beside[s] Eric getting revenge and grieving his dead fiancée. It is very simple and very disappointing." The post has 109

---

82 R/movies on Reddit, "The Crow is bad. Really bad.," accessed May 3, 2024, https://www.reddit.com/r/movies/comments/vdv2bq/the_crow_is_bad_really_bad/.

comments with many people roasting the original poster alive for sharing their opinion. Some agree with the post, saying that the fight scenes are trash or that the film doesn't hold up. One person says that there is nothing wrong with liking simple storytelling, while another goes through the post bit by bit trying to explain to the original poster why they are wrong, with another saying, "You are fucking insane, *The Crow* is the best comic book movie ever made." It is interesting to read this post simply because the original poster doesn't make a single mention of Lee; there is no talk of irony, no scepter. It's just a person who didn't like the film.

A few people on Rotten Tomatoes also echo Anderson Jones's sentiment from 1994, saying that more than being the reason for why people like the film, Lee's death overshadows what is actually not a great movie. "A movie that has remained in the cultural zeitgeist largely because of the lead actor's tragic death, not because the final product was actualy [*sic*] anything memorable," writes Rotten Tomatoes user Nate H.

A review from 2014 on a site called *Montreal Film Journal* faults the film for, again, simplicity of screenplay and dreadful and unoriginal dialogue. The reviewer notes that Eric is "well interpreted by Brandon Lee (who died during the shoot)" and that "he looks way cool with face painting." Nonetheless, the film is "just so B," no better than a straight-to-video B-horror "no one ever hears of because their star didn't die during a scene."[83]

---

[83] Moore Lamarre, "The Crow," *Montreal Film Journal*, October 24, 2014, https://montrealfilmjournal.com/the-crow/.

The passage of time seems to have removed the fog of irony for these reviewers.

These reviews, posts, and comments stratify the three kinds of responses to *The Crow* that seem to be most common. In the first camp belong the die-hard fans, myself included. We attend screenings where we might dress up as Eric Draven. We have the special edition of the comic book and so many film-related t-shirts. (Have I told you about my Hangman's Joke t-shirt?) In the second camp are those who point to the irony of a movie about death that precipitated the lead actor's literal death, like so many of the reviewers in 1994. And thirdly, there are those who make it a point to look at the film apart from the tragedy that overshadows it.

## HOW TO MAKE FRIENDS AND STILL TALK ABOUT *THE CROW*

There's a problem with how we talk about Brandon Lee and *The Crow*.

Pressman hoped that Lee's death would become "less interesting than the movie itself. The point is not to remind people of the tragedy." But Ascher-Walsh is astute in noticing that this would be tough: "Any audience will have trouble separating Lee's fate from that of his character. But lest anyone forget what was lost, there is a final, unmistakeable reminder in the simple dedication at the movie's end: 'For Brandon and Eliza.'"

I think a lot of interpretations of *The Crow*, past and present, graft tragedy onto the past, onto the whole of the film, and onto Lee, to the extent that we see a man like the figure he played, weeping and brooding and moody, a man doomed from the start and sulking toward the doom; we see the man only inasmuch as we see *The Crow* and the events that took place. But the truth is always so much more complicated and full than the simplicity of words, flat labels that they are. The truth is that Brandon Lee was a man madly in love with life and excited about marriage. He loved waxing poetic and philosophical, and he was unafraid to be ridiculous. He was multi-layered, as we all are. He was a person.

"I've learned as I've gotten a little older, that it just doesn't do anybody any good for you to get hurt on a film, because it just slows everything down," he told Wygant. "It costs everybody a lot of money, and it puts a lot of people out of work. It's not a particularly responsible thing to do." These are pragmatic words, professional, understanding that, after all, he is working when he steps onto a set, not hoping to fulfill some sort of prophecy. He had goals: his immediate one was to get married, but he also wanted to make a film depicting fight scenes in a raw manner, not theatricalized and glamorized, that was grounded in reality, striking a register close to street fighting. He wanted to work across many genres, too.

It's tiresome to constantly harp on the "eerie-ness" of the similarities between his passing and his father's passing, between his end and the tragedy that informs O'Barr's story. This kind of reading is certainly enticing (we do, after all, tell ourselves stories to survive, to understand the messy, uncontrollable around us — it's instinctive), but I wish we would take a step back once in a while. A reading of an entire lived life that transplants fiction onto that life also transplants a certain fatalism and robs a person of their will, flattening their hopes, dreams, and goals, their right to make mistakes, to be mercurial, and all the various contradictory things they thought and said and did. To read Lee's accident within the clean confines of the narrative centralizes his death, which is horrendous and without empathy; the accident should not have happened, it could have been avoided through responsible management. It should have been avoided.

\*

Is it possible to consider *The Crow* in a vacuum? Is it morally permissible? Can you ever mention it without also talking about tragedy? I don't think so, and I don't know if I would want to, even if I wish that Brandon Lee's death could be considered with a measure of sobriety and less as a bedrock for circuitous irony. The thing about art is that it helps us feel less alone while it makes sense of our misery, anguish, and happiness. The film begins with Sarah's narration: "Sometimes, something so bad happens that The Crow can bring that soul back to put the wrong things right." Ascher-Walsh says that Sarah's words and the film could help others feel less "wrong" by carrying the hopes of the entire cast and crew into the world in the form of Eric Draven or Brandon Lee, both brought back to life every time we press play or go to the theater, trying to put the wrong things right. Many said that Lee would have been proud of the final product. I would be remiss if I recommended that a person forget about his passing while watching the film; indeed, it's virtually impossible.

O'Barr has said time and time again that the story of Eric and Shelly is one about love, so why do so many focus only on the literal deaths surrounding the story? Why do they overshadow or obfuscate the message of enduring love, one so powerful it pulls us back from the dead?

*

*The Crow*, first a graphic novel and then a film, delivers the narrative of its literal death by being grounded within humanity. In James O'Barr's case, this means that the pain he felt at losing Beverly could not subside on its own, aching like the pounding throb of a fresh cut. Instead, it needed to be released into his art, to live within the pages of his graphic novel. O'Barr dealt with literal death through creation; it was then that he could move through grief and stay alive. The film's literal death is also the story of Brandon Lee deeply empathizing with O'Barr's pain and living through grief and death on screen, both scripted and also, tragically, not. The film did not anticipate his real-life death, but the work he did to understand death has left behind a glimmering scaffolding for the sadness caused by his passing; we have, thanks to him, a more freeing way to process such weighty loss. And it is only alongside this, within the context of both O'Barr's and Lee's work, the life on paper and then on screen, that *The Crow*'s literal death can also be about the end of Lee's life.

Grounded in human pain, O'Barr and Lee offer us two distinct and connected works of art that are alive despite the deaths inherent in their stories. This has been the story of how they packaged and gifted us with the cliché, the familiar, and the resonant.

# part two
# visceral life

# 3

## Breathed to Life

FOCUS ON THE SELF

Brandon Lee doesn't really care about *The Crow*'s themes, none of its holistic or overarching messages.

"I'll tell you something, I don't really care about any statements the film makes," Lee says frankly near the end of *The Crow* featurette. "Because that's not Eric's point of view. I'm sure that the world of this film is going to be a better place once the bad guys aren't there anymore, but that's not Eric's reason for doing what he's doing, so it's not something I've stopped to consider a great deal."

All of *The Crow*'s power comes from Eric's focus, involuntary though it is, on the self, and Lee understands this. Eric's story is a selfish one and, therefore, deeply human. "Eric gets the chance to come back and try and see that some kind of justice is done," Lee says. "It's not necessarily a pretty subject, but it's one that I feel comes from him very organically, and it's quite justified," Lee says of the film's violence, the mode through which Eric strives toward his own idea of justice.

For Eric, feelings and memories have menacing proportions. As soon as Eric touches Gabriel, he is yanked into the moment of his and Shelly's deaths. The memory knocks him to his knees, not so much from the pain he felt at being shot and falling but from the act of memory itself — the memories seem to have their own mind and weight as they charge through his body. When he's attacking Tin Tin and he asks him if he remembers Shelly, Tin Tin admits he remembers raping and killing her, a statement from which Eric winces before he slaps him in the face. When Eric touches Albrecht's forehead to see what the officer saw of Shelly in her final moments at the hospital, the force of her pain, which Albrecht only witnessed, knocks Eric down again. Eric shows no abashedness or restraint when it comes to the past; he feels it with the same immediacy the present holds.

*Comes from him organically*, Lee says of the violence. All of Eric is unmediated. The action in *The Crow* flows from Eric, who doesn't *allow* his feelings — anger, sadness, physical and psychic pain — to surface; rather he fully *becomes* them, without fear or care. What he generates, in turn, are acts of pure revenge and throbbing love. And all of this is selfish in the sense that Eric is not, as Lee says, concerned with making the world a better place but with making himself feel better. All that we see of Eric comes from him organically.

*

As Proyas's lens hovers and roves over a dark city caught perennially between drowning in rain and sparking ablaze, Sarah's narration at the film's beginning describes a soul in torment: "People once believed that when someone dies, a crow carries their soul to the land of the dead. But sometimes, something so bad happens that a terrible sadness is carried with it [the soul], and the soul can't rest. Then sometimes — just sometimes — The Crow can bring that soul back to put the wrong things right."

Eric is brought back a year after the accident, and one imagines his soul stuck in limbo during that time, thrashing and wailing and screaming, going mad from the vile injustice of what has happened to him and Shelly. When The Crow comes to Eric's grave, it raps on his gravestone like the raven in Edgar Allan Poe's classic and often quoted poem "The Raven," which has always seemed to me to encapsulate a kind of hell of helplessness, the kind Eric crawls out of with a scream that tears through the screen.

I have always thought "The Raven" to be about distraction, the futility of keeping oneself distracted from an abysmal sadness. It begins with the protagonist, the "I," nodding off at midnight over towering volumes of "forgotten lore" in an attempt to "vainly" borrow from them a surcease of sorrow over a deceased love, Lenore.[84] A rapping at the narrator's door jolts him awake. He's afraid at first, like Eric flinching from The Crow when he first awakens. A raven eventually flies through the door and lands on a sculpted bust: "Perched, and sat, and nothing more." For the rest of the poem, the raven merely sits and repeats "Nevermore" again and again as the narrator is nearly driven insane.

Poe's poem is as lonesome and yearning as O'Barr's novel and the film, all three equally exploring and exposing the hellish landscape of grief. For O'Barr, the black bird is a soul carrier and guardian; for Poe, the raven is, as it is in much of literature, a harbinger of doom. But both birds also serve as necessary distractions.

In the book and film, Eric is helplessly stuck in pain until The Crow comes. The Crow swoops in and pulls Eric onto the plane of the living so that he can find peace. In Poe's version, the narrator is futilely looking for a distraction from thinking about his lost love — one can only imagine how tired he must be of feeling so sad all the time. When the bird arrives, the narrator is pulled out of himself and, on the evidence of his grand and frenetic gestures around the bird, seems grateful for it: he reflexively becomes an apologetic host, enticed by the prospect of a guest, and when he sees his caller is a bird, he too easily, without a self-conscious thought, throws himself into all-consuming concentration as he tries to figure the raven out. Though his focus seems

---

84 Edgar Allan Poe, "Miscellaneous Poems," essay, in *Edgar Allan Poe: Complete Tales & Poems* (Castle Books, 2002).

exaggerated, it also seems genuine, like a person quick to laugh after a crying spell or one pressing on the bruise of a smashed finger — the bigger the feeling, the better the distraction. He haphazardly drags a chair to his doorstep and sits, concentrating on the bird with jocularity that swiftly devolves into anger at the raven's metaphysical meaning — all of the narrator's action in the poem is, to me, like Eric's vengeance. The narrator literally ponders a bird and becomes pondering personified. It's absurd, but like Eric's violence, it's all he can do that might help him to feel better, for the alternative is painful rumination.

Both The Crow and the raven are mystical figures who offer a measure of peace because they allow a breather during the mourning process through their companionship. They walk their humans toward the tough work that needs to be done, helping them take the first step outside their circling minds and toward something productive for no one but themselves, something that might lessen their unique burdens of loneliness. In the land of the living, they can confront what ails them, finally and for better or worse.

Many years lie between Poe's poem and O'Barr's novel and film, and yet these works of art capture the same ideas: the discomfort in confronting death and loss, grief itself, and our instinct to distract ourselves from the task of processing it. This comparison illuminates the timeless energy of grief as well as the timelessness of *The Crow* itself.

✳

"The Raven" and *The Crow* make legible the tendency in their humans to simultaneously become obsessed with their pain and desperately avoid entanglement with it. In the film, the act of touch functions in the same way — it both beckons and repels. Nothing about Eric is anchored in a cool and calculating rationality; rather, all of his thinking and actions come from the hot, flashing, and vibrant realm of his feeling, from the whipping and foaming anger and sadness he feels. It comes from the gooey, visceral, alive part of him. Accordingly, one of his powers, in addition to temporary immortality granted him for two nights, is the ability to *know* immediately through touch. It's a kind of instant empathy or hyper/surreal intuition, tragic simply for the fact that for Eric, all that's communicated is pain and hurt: memories of sweetness with Shelly, whose happiness is so blinding it sears, and her and his pain before death.

When Eric touches Gabriel the cat, the memories flood back, and he keels over in pain. Touch in this film is a powerful communicator, which is apt for a film that deals with feeling, not logic. It's something unique to the film — in O'Barr's novel, Eric doesn't possess such a power. Throughout the film, Eric's memories of his life are jogged as he touches people he once knew, like Sarah, or who have empathy, like Albrecht. He also fills gaps in his memory through touch; as he touches the gang members, he gets a better understanding of what happened the night he and Shelly died. Every time he remembers through touch, it's as painful as a cracked tooth. For example, when he picks Sarah up off the street because she is about to skateboard into the path of an oncoming car, her memory of watching Shelly try on wedding dresses sticks to him with the immediacy and force of iron to a magnet, causing Eric to drop her unceremoniously onto the sidewalk. This pain, with its own electric life, is exactly why graphic-novel-Eric cuts himself because physical pain is better than the memories that course through his mind according to their own whim. A bleeding hand or a finger throbbing from the pain of a door slam is a much less torturous experience than memories of paradise lost.

Memories become physical tokens, and at the film's end, Eric uses this weighty knowledge to his advantage during his final battle with Top Dollar. Eric is about to lose a physical duel with Top, who is close to killing him, which would have uncertain consequences for his immortal fate. At the last minute, Eric places his hands over Top's face, declaring he has something for him, and passes along Shelly's pain, which immobilizes Top and causes him to fall to his death. It's such a heartbreaking way to overpower a combatant, especially for Lee, who, in other cases (in other films and for other villains in *The Crow*), uses his physicality, acumen, and skill to win. It's fitting that what destroys the film's towering villain is exactly what has been torturing its hero: the death of his lover.

In the film's final moments, as Eric lies losing consciousness over Shelly's grave after he has accomplished his goal, she materializes and touches Eric. This is the first time in the afterlife that touch doesn't hurt him. Eric is awakened gently by Shelly's tender touch, and it finally brings him calm and peace. He is with his beloved forevermore.

## THE HOT, VISCERAL, ALIVE PART OF HIM

Nothing about Eric comes from a rational place that weighs the good against the bad, the pros against the cons. All of his action — the fights, his decision to burn photos of Shelly, the way he jerks between emotions — contains an immediacy and fluidity with no hesitation. The eagerness with which he plunges into vengeful danger is breathtakingly foolhardy. When he introduces himself to his first kill, Tin Tin, he throws himself off the side of a building into a formidable pile of trash. It's the first time we get a full view of his painted face, and never has there been a more badass entrance. But it's also uncalculated and self-destructive. Eric literally throws himself into trash and then gets up nonchalantly. It's not an objectively utilitarian thing to do, and it doesn't feel like it's something Eric planned. It's not for show, either, for Tin Tin doesn't see him fall; nobody sees him fall except for The Crow.

It seems as though he would act with the same passion even if he weren't granted immortality, and he does. By the film's end, he begins to lose his immortality when The Crow is injured and taken from him by Top Dollar. He begins to feel pain and bleed, and yet he still tells the gun-wielding Albrecht to stay behind him so that he will be safe, even though Eric himself will not be. He is noble here, but logistically foolish; reason always takes a back seat for Eric, for whom feelings of love and anger and sadness are most important and worth honoring. They drip off of him with the same reality as the perennial rain.

I am always confounded by those who say that the film's script and trajectory are simplistic, who complain that this is a mere and bare revenge tale. *The Crow* is emotionally rich and charged, unhinged from the brittle laws of logic. Eric is unpredictable, frightening, and intensely loving — all things that are far removed from, indeed polar opposite to, the heartless logic and traditional, binary, and linear notions of how a man, and a traditional film, ought to be. If Eric is renegade and revolutionary because of his emotional unabashedness, then it stands to reason that a film with him at its center is equally revolutionary and not simplistic at all.

## THE GRUNGE ETHOS

The 1980s in the U.S. saw, under the election of deeply conservative Ronald Reagan as president, a hard and uncompromising stratification and polarization of gender roles within mainstream culture. Much of this stratification was in response to the sexual revolution and the women's rights movement of the '60s.[85] Pulitzer Prize–winning writer Susan Faludi penned *Backlash: The Undeclared War Against American Women* in 1991, a searing and thorough look at the backlash against women's rights, specifically under the Reagan administration.

---

85 Françoise Coste, "'Women, Ladies, Girls, Gals…': Ronald Reagan and the Evolution of Gender Roles in the United States," *Miranda*, no. 12 (February 24, 2016), https://doi.org/10.4000/miranda.8602.

As more and more women entered the workforce, the '80s giddily and loudly declared that "the struggle for women's rights is won," Faludi writes. At the same time, though, mainstream media peddled tales of women's woes relating to workplace burnout. It was being feverishly reported that working too much could lead a woman to "hair loss, bad nerves, alcoholism, and even heart attacks," which in turn could cause infertility issues.[86] Stories of women experiencing work-related burnout symptoms — a newsworthy topic as the number of women working outside the home increased to unprecedented numbers — both daunted women and emboldened the anti-feminism movement.

How could it be that, despite having won the fight for women's rights, women were still so miserable? "The prevailing wisdom of the past decade has supported one, and only one, answer to this riddle: it must be that equality that's causing all the pain," Faludi wrote from the vantage point of the '90s.[87] A spokesperson for Reagan called feminism a "straightjacket" for women. For Reagan-era conservatives, men and women had their distinct roles: men belonged in the workplace while women belonged in the home.[88] Burnout symptoms were rationalized as the inevitable fatigue of a body unfit for the same labor as men. Ideology is a hell of a drug.

---

86 Susan Faludi, *Backlash: The Undeclared War against Women* (Broadway Books, 2020).

87 Ibid.

88 Françoise Coste, "'Women, Ladies, Girls, Gals...': Ronald Reagan and the Evolution of Gender Roles in the United States," *Miranda*, no. 12 (February 24, 2016), https://doi.org/10.4000/miranda.8602.

In many films and television shows produced by Hollywood in the '80s, the (sexually, sociopolitically) liberated woman often would either be reformed from or punished for her ambition. She would end a story dead, in jail, or subdued within the arms of a dashing, strong, manly man, a clarion reflection of Reagan's own image in Hollywood in the '50s. As an actor, he was marketed by Warner Bros. as "the all-American heterosexual hero, 'tall and handsome,' with 'nothing of the pretty boy about him' since 'virility [was] his outstanding characteristic.'"[89]

Reagan didn't invent misogyny, but he was its loudest and most powerful proponent in a culture anxious about women gaining autonomy. A successful film like 1985's *Jagged Edge* visualizes its male creators' anxiety about a working woman, played by Glenn Close, who might take their jobs. Close plays a successful lawyer but a bad mother; she is, of course, going through a divorce. Throughout the film, she is slammed (through dialogue or metaphorically) for neglecting her kids. Lacking childcare — or discouraged from accessing it — she takes her kids with her to meet a potentially dangerous client at the film's start, and the story frames this decision as shameful. And 1987's *Fatal Attraction*, another Glenn Close movie, vocalizes its male creator Adrian Lyne's anxieties about the cruel and cold working woman who doesn't have a family. This woman, predictably, destroys the domestic bliss of a successful married man. Close does a brilliant job in both films, but her characters

---

89 Ibid.

are still the creations of men in the '80s who were preoccupied with power and the threat of women.

There were very real women who worked outside of the home and came home afterward to perform the more invisible domestic labor that men did not, and they often faced a unique kind of burnout from this unabating work. Women who were depicted in media as doing both forms of labor and not complaining were seen as "having it all" (or, more aptly put, "doing" it all). They never seemed tired, which, as we all know, was simply impossible. If a TV show like *Family Ties* depicted a woman both working professionally and doing domestic labor happily, then the implication was that this immense workload was healthily possible (which it wasn't and isn't), but it also intimated that a woman did not need "liberation" any longer. She already had it all and didn't need anything else, said this variant of feminist backlash.

This is not to say that there were no positive representations in media of women enjoying success in the workplace and happiness at home. But feminism faced a multi-pronged attack from a mainstream capitalist and patriarchal culture, which presented unforgiving images of the right and wrong ways to be. An impossible pressure was placed on women. Some women thought they shouldn't kowtow to capitalism, while others were told to work doubly, while others, I'm sure, must have felt like bad feminists for staying at home.

The backlash to this backlash was scattered throughout the counterculture in art and music on the fringes of the mainstream. As is counterculture's wont, it vocalized people's disdain for the mostly boring and often violent imposition of the gender binary by making space for alternative expressions of the self. When James O'Barr was creating *The Crow*, the music he was drawn to, that he chose to alleviate and articulate his grief, also happened to exemplify the counterculture's penchant for dismantling the status quo. The aching lyrics of Joy Division, the deeply moody '80s band that was a direct precursor to today's EDM, are littered throughout the comic book and helped O'Barr feel validated in his pain through a sound that is "lush and tonally rich" and words that are "doomy and angry."[90] Helmed by Ian Curtis, who grew "this image of a depressed reclusive gloomy romantic hero," the band telegraphed a sensitive masculinity in stark contrast to the mainstream.[91] "Produced under Thatcherism and Reaganism amid the Cold War, deepening social inequality, and the rise of the surveillance state, songs like "Disorder," "Dead Souls," "Atrocity Exhibition," and "Isolation" exude disquiet and alienation. They could have been written today," writes culture scholar David Rowe.[92]

Nine Inch Nails cover "Dead Souls" for the film's soundtrack, while the chapter in the graphic novel depicting the lovers' murders is called "The Atrocity Exhibition." Eric,

---

[90] David Rowe, "Will Time Tear Us Apart? Exploring the Appeal of Joy Division 40 Years On," *The Conversation*, August 2, 2019, https://theconversation.com/will-time-tear-us-apart-exploring-the-appeal-of-joy-division-40-years-on-121314.

[91] Peter Kenworthy, "Joy Division and Ian Curtis: The Myths," *New Internationalist*, June 6, 2018, https://newint.org/features/web-exclusive/2018/06/01/joy-division-ian-curtis.

[92] David Rowe, "Will Time Tear Us Apart? Exploring the Appeal of Joy Division 40 Years On." *The Conversation*, August 2, 2019, https://theconversation.com/will-time-tear-us-apart-exploring-the-appeal-of-joy-division-40-years-on-121314.

meanwhile, emerges as a nimble and sensitive gothic figure, paying homage to Peter Murphy and Iggy Pop — radically feminine in the context of Reagan's strict dichotomy.

*

By the time *The Crow* was being adapted for the screen, 1990s grunge took center stage as the "It" countercultural movement of the times, bottling a lot of the fluidity that O'Barr's favorite music, like Joy Division, wrangled. Grunge's poster child is Nirvana lead vocalist, songwriter, and guitarist Kurt Cobain, who epitomized a particular kind of grunge ethos that found immense resonance.

"He was so kind, and so worried about people, if they were okay, or if somebody got hurt," Cobain's mother Wendy says in *Kurt Cobain: Montage of Heck*, an insightful 2015 documentary that charts his life. Cobain was a deeply empathetic person who was acutely aware of others' feelings. In his suicide note, he wrote of feeling "too sensitive."[93]

> I need to be slightly numb in order to regain the enthusiasms I once had as a child. On our last 3 tours, I've had a much better appreciation for all the people I've known personally, and as fans of our music, but I still can't get over the frustration, the guilt and empathy I have for everyone. There's good in all of us and I think I simply

---

[93] Marco Margaritoff, "Inside the Text of Kurt Cobain's Heartwrenching Suicide Note," *All That's Interesting*, June 10, 2024, https://allthatsinteresting.com/kurt-cobain-suicide-note.

love people too much, so much that it makes me feel too fucking sad.[94]

I've often felt this way — rendered inefficient in the world by a debilitating empathy, always aching like an exposed nerve in a brisk breeze, walking through the world feeling like a purple bruise. This kind of empathy sprouts an effusion of feeling, which often leaves me and people like me out of step with the cycles of productivity inherent in a capitalist patriarchy. To be in the state of feeling is, I have written, "not so much navel gazing as it is a listening to and honoring of, and potentially acting on one's feelings, for better or for worse."[95] It's all action stemming from internal ache, from empathy or sympathy or psychic pain, as opposed to the cool and rational and planned action that capitalism requires of us. And this kind of feeling is what Cobain embodied in his music in the early '90s.

Grunge is often loosely described sonically as having a distorted soundscape and "heartfelt and anguished lyrics."[96] Cobain's iteration of grunge, effectively amplifying his aching empathy, was specifically feminist. In a diary entry depicted in *Montage of Heck*, Cobain writes one of his foundational rules:

---

94 Ibid.

95 Alisha Mughal, "The Weight of Feeling: How 'The Crow' and 'John Wick' Embody Kurt Cobain's Grunge Image," *Film Daze*, October 28, 2023, https://filmdaze.net/the-weight-of-feeling-how-the-crow-and-john-wick-embody-kurt-cobains-grunge-image/.

96 Jacklyn Grambush, "A Brief History of Grunge: The Seattle Sound," Culture Trip, April 9, 2019, https://theculturetrip.com/north-america/usa/washington/articles/a-brief-history-of-grunge-the-seattle-sound.

a woman ought never to be hurt while playing a gig or otherwise. He actively didn't care about traditional gender norms. He often wore dresses in public, and his lyrics were lush, all up in his feels. Through his public persona, he offered a fluid and elastic version of masculinity, receptive even as it held space in society. I've written that Cobain "projected a kind of safe presence that wasn't domineering, but was rather respectful of goodness and self-aware as it made its case against a bitter and exclusionary status quo."[97]

In her seminal essay "Kurt Cobain Pushed the Boundaries of Gender and Made Room for Us All," writer Niko Stratis describes Cobain's particular brand of anger and intense feeling:

> [His was n]ot an anger misplaced, mind you, but an anger languishing in abstraction. I always felt that Cobain, like myself and indeed a lot of people, was vainly attempting to pinpoint the things within himself that felt out of step with the world around him. He wasn't angry at a system or a woman who had wronged him. He was frustrated, seeking an unattainable sense of control over himself, his own pain, and his place in the world.[98]

---

[97] Alisha Mughal, "The Weight of Feeling How 'The Crow' and 'John Wick' Embody Kurt Cobain's Grunge Image," *Film Daze*, October 28, 2023, https://filmdaze.net/the-weight-of-feeling-how-the-crow-and-john-wick-embody-kurt-cobains-grunge-image/.

[98] Niko Stratis, "Kurt Cobain Pushed the Boundaries of Gender and Made Room for Us All," *Catapult*, March 1, 2022, https://magazine.catapult.co/column/stories/niko-stratis-everyone-is-gay-nirvana-kurt-cobain-pushed-boundaries-gender-masculinity-queerness-rock-grunge.

Within Cobain, there was a miasma of feeling, an "internal strife" that waged publicly, readable on his person and in his lyrics. In his allowance of feeling, in baring it all, Stratis writes, he challenged and frustrated traditional gender norms, even as he was pained by them. Accordingly, Stratis writes, he set it all ablaze:

> The most striking thing about Cobain, outside of the flannel-clad bluster and bravado of grunge, was how he pushed the boundaries of his gender. He would regularly appear onstage wearing a dress over his usual attire of jeans and multiple shirts. As time wore on between the massive success of *Nevermind* and follow-up album *In Utero*, he seemed to revel in being seen as anything but what was codified as your average cishet man.[99]

With Cobain, we have a person not only rejecting the dictates of traditional (Reaganite) masculinity (which expects men to suppress feelings and subjugate women) but also a figure who so compellingly represents the countercultural core of grunge. Cobain felt unabashedly and, therefore, radically, communicating his feelings through his bleeding words and wearing his heart on his sleeve. He was everything a man, according to traditional notions, ought not to be.

*

---

[99] Ibid.

Eric Draven is an open wound, bleeding out an overwhelming immensity of feeling in a manner quite redolent of Kurt Cobain. Eric represents Cobain's focus on the self, the vanity that frustrates and arrests; Eric embodies Cobain's flailing within a cold and cruel world as he reveals along the way an inability or unwillingness to suppress feeling, to hide pain or sadness. Eric is a bleeding heart, like Cobain, possessing an effusion of feeling that traditional notions consider feminine, and he, like Cobain, works not so much to fix the system (the world around him) as he does to simply exist and feel, to do whatever it takes to feel better within himself. Any fixing of the world — Cobain standing up for feminism and making space for others, Eric ridding the world of bad guys — is secondary, a by-product of both men's impassioned existences. Self-oriented, Eric's anger is, as Stratis says Cobain's is, "not an anger misplaced, mind you, but an anger languishing in abstraction." An anger allowed to languish unchecked.

Cobain wished to numb his pain so that he could focus on the world, but this is, of course, impossible. Eric is also trapped within his subjectivity, moving to the beat of an unignorable pain, hewed forcibly to its truth. And by virtue of his feelings, he bucks traditional notions and behaviors associated with toxic masculinity. He displays a Cobain-esque tender masculinity, acting to fulfill his desires and, if not release, then underscore his pains through screams and violence. This is why Brandon Lee never cared about *The Crow*'s sociopolitical themes; he understood that Eric doesn't care to fix the system, he just wants to alleviate his own pain, however futile this may be. He simply wants to soothe his soul.

For all of Eric's outward presentation of traditionally masculine strength (muscular build, his guns and swords), it is stunning how Lee manages to infuse something so tender into him, translating the earlier decade's counterculture O'Barr baked into the character. Lee is unafraid to move his body, yielding his towering, strong form to flighty and changeable feelings as gracefully as a dancer, reveling in the kind of fluidity that an average cishet man, constrained by the imposing and persuasive strictures of traditional masculinity, would be terrified of performing. Eric beautifully embodies Cobain's grunge-y soul. Inasmuch as Eric's real tragedy is that he learns that his pain is uncontrollable, it's also a blessing, for it leaves him eternally alive.

## "YOU'RE JUST GOING TO HAVE TO FORGIVE ME FOR THAT"

In the way that so many of America's ailments — a rehabilitated conservatism; a war on drugs that financially benefits the prison industrial complex and overwhelmingly persecutes and prosecutes marginalized people; trickle-down economics and modern-day capitalism; the entrenchment of anti-gay sentiments and violence in conservative ideology; a cottage industry of international weapons dealing — can be traced back to the Reagan administration, many of Western society's norms can be traced back to Plato.

In *Republic*, Plato has Socrates ascertain and illustrate what justice is. Socrates arrives at an image of justice as a harmony in the soul: it is when each part or aspect of a person's soul performs its function. The soul is divided into three parts: the appetitive (appetites and bodily desires), the spirited (passions, such as anger or shame), and the rational. It is the role of reason to lead and of the spirited part to, in alliance with and under reason's guidance, keep watch over the appetites, which must never run amok, certainly never rule. Justice is when the ruler rules and the ruled parts remain ruled, especially the bodily appetites.

In a book called *The Flight to Objectivity: Essays on Cartesianism and Culture*, American philosopher Susan Bordo bridges the gap between Plato and modernity by outlining how patriarchal culture arrived at its mind-body dualism. "Platonic and neo-Platonic thought, and the Christian traditions that grew out of them, all exhibit" a disdain for the body, a disdain that is yanked into modernity by French philosopher René Descartes.[100] Descartes, armed with a Platonic understanding of the functions of soul and body, would take things a step further and define the mind and body as mutually exclusive. While for Plato, it is possible to live well with a body if the appetites are under the control of reason, for Descartes, it is possible to transcend the body altogether, to live a life without any care for the body at all,

---

[100] Susan Bordo, *The Flight to Objectivity: Essays on Cartesianism and Culture* (SUNY Press, 1987).

meaning that subjectivity can be overcome to attain pure objectivity. After Plato and Descartes, and following the currents of the development of science and industry, "impersonality has become the mark of the truth of the known," writes Bordo.[101]

When we think about truth today, we think of science that doesn't favor or denigrate any specific people. The truth has nothing particular or unique about it, nothing about space and time to mark it; it will always be universal, eternally abiding. The earth, the earthly, is analogous to the body, ever-changing, under the sway of time and space, while the mind, because it *can* attain objectivity, is analogous to objective science. The strict and clean rules of science, reason codified, provide the rules that attempt to govern the mercurial material world, not the other way around. This thinking, this conflict of subjective and objective, or body and mind, with objective/mind over-valued, more than trickled into culture — it shaped Western conscience (not to mention Christian ideology); dealing in oughts and ought-nots, these thinkers were talking about the "right," or the most truthful way to be.

This divide, the patriarchy's understanding of mind and body, is most clearly represented in the modern healthcare system: the body and women who are seen as trapped within their bodies have been considered "voracious" and "insatiable," earthly and subjective, and need to be controlled by objective science, or objective masculinity.[102] Women's bodies are not

---

101 Ibid.

102 Ibid.

considered in their own right but with reference to the rules of science, made to fit its confines when they stray, when they assert their subjectivity.

The male body has long been considered the standard in medicine, leaving many aspects of women's health, such as menopause, under-researched. Up until very recently, autism was defined and described with regard to how it manifested in men, going mostly undetected and underdiagnosed in women; its presentation in women is only now being studied. (This is also beautifully spelled out by Barbara Ehrenreich and Dierdre English in 1973's *Witches, Midwives, and Nurses*.) Plato's and then Descartes's gigantic shadows still loom heavily over the Western patriarchal understanding of truth and gender, of the "right" way to be: objective mind/reason ruling over the unruly and subjective body, objective men ruling over women, and others mired in their subjectivities.

Fast forward to the early 1990s, after thousands of years of patriarchy and emotionless toxic masculinity, and Kurt Cobain's gender-bucking presence appears, with his movement between the traditionally masculine to the territory of the "other" and his subsequent occupation of space outside and between the oughts and ought-nots. He was radical, critical of, and caustic about heteronormativity.

\*

In the face of all this, Eric Draven strikes a register defiantly alongside Cobain. He is all subjectivity and emotion, he lives in his body, honoring his needs and desires. He is the fool, a selfish one, the trickster crow taking center stage. In an exciting turn, O'Barr and the film elevate the auxiliary trope of The Fool, a character defined as having no distinct goal or idea of what they're doing, to the enigmatic protagonist.[103] The Fool traditionally has a vague grasp of their enemies and friends as they stumble blissfully blinkered through the plot as comic relief, protected only by their cheerful disposition and the blessing of Lady Luck. In medieval plays, The Fool would be a stand-in for the audience, or the average civilian; a kind of trickster, he would get to be King for a single day at the annual Feast of Fools, a kind of parody of ecclesiastical ritual, and a kind of joke on The Fool, too.[104] For two nights in *The Crow*, the resurrected Eric looms large and menacing as a complicated Fool, a haunted and damned joker, a depressed and doomed Don Quixote, elevated to the status of vengeful savior, a king, if you will, of vigilante justice. In O'Barr's story, the two-night-long rampage is also a dark sort of joke on Eric, who learns only at the end that peace does not lie in justified murder but in self-forgiveness.

*The Crow* does complicated and very interesting things with The Fool, fleshing him out and frustrating him. Eric is a fool for love; indeed, his existence within the world of the movie is foolish. He feels and loves and cares in a way that isn't meaningful to anyone — not Top Dollar's criminal system, nor

---

103 "The Fool," TV Tropes, accessed May 3, 2024, https://tvtropes.org/pmwiki/pmwiki.php/Main/TheFool.

104 Ibid.

straight society's productivity. So much of Eric's thrashing, his violence in the name of love, is like Don Quixote attacking a windmill. Eric has been dead for a year, and to come back from the afterlife to avenge his and Shelly's deaths only to die once again seems meaningless. But, of course, it's not meaningless.

Eric's sadness — though it holds no currency in the physical realm where rationality and logic are valued — is shown by Lee to be as weighty as the sea. Nothing is trivial, smoking will kill you, Eric tells Albrecht — and this matters; it mattered to Shelly and it now matters to him in death. Don Quixote believes that the windmills are giants; he believes in his love, and when a belief is strong, all else pales in importance, and so the windmills need to be attacked. Eric feels pain and anger and agony, and all of these things, these *feelings* and *passions* that exist in his body, that are uniquely his, though invisible, hurt and sear more than any physical wound can. Rather than force them to come under the rule of his reason, Eric lets his feelings and passions rule; reason has no place in Eric's afterlife. Lee says in the featurette that after a year of being dead, everyone in Eric's world will have moved on, but Eric doesn't care. Everyone will die because Eric is sad.

If The Fool is blissfully unaware, then Eric is untethered from any other consideration by his blinkered goal, caring for nothing other than his pain and Shelly and revenge. With his care for himself centered within his memories and emotions, he neglects his bodily welfare, leaving it in the care of The Crow as he throws himself into violence. He stands motionless in front of a storm of bullets that Top Dollar's gang members fire down on him, simply waiting for it to end, just so he can get to and kill Skank — he knows that The Crow will protect him, will ensure his momentary immortality. He tumbles headlong into his adversaries' guns, laughing maniacally in evil's face and, therefore, terrifyingly.

Eric is aware of his forlorn, ridiculous position in the same way that The Fool has no grandiose aspirations and knows he is only a fake king for a singular day. Eric knows very well that he will never live alongside Shelly on the earthly plane and will never get married in the real world, but this doesn't matter to him. Not once does he wonder about bringing Shelly back to life. All he cares to do is seek revenge because his soul is in so much pain, it blinds him; he will take his second life to avenge the wrong done unto him, avenge the theft of his beautiful love, the ruination of his life. He doesn't once speak of rejoining Shelly in the afterlife, either, as if he hasn't thought of his immortal future yet. He is all immediacy, a dead man killing.

Eric also maintains The Fool's sense of the comical — he cracks jokes left, right, and center, dancing and jumping around with a playfulness and mirth that on his sad figure scan as garish and grim, all the more doomed. Moreover, Eric is preternaturally intelligent, waxing poetic every chance he gets, quoting Gothic and Decadent poets gleefully, his moody, bleeding heart punctuating punches, pontificating as he rains bloody violence on the gang who wronged him. And his poetic and musical bent is self-serving, too, just for him. No one in his world appreciates his jokes, anyway. He plays his guitar, the one audiences laugh at him for picking up at the pawn shop, on the roof of his building — maybe because it feels right, maybe because it reminds him of Shelly — as the city burns beneath him, and then he just smashes it, destroys the instrument when he is done with it, maybe because it feels right, maybe because it reminds him too much of Shelly.

*

The physical transference, carriage, and honoring of memories and feelings are some of this film's greatest gifts. I've tried so often in the past to shake heavy memories off, but it never works; I've cowered and covered my head with my hands, but that doesn't stop them, either. This film seems to understand that sometimes, memories and emotions feel as real as any physical object. When Eric hurls himself out of his apartment window, mimicking the manner in which he died, and the glass pierces him like stigmata, the pain has him look at his hands, and he is horrified to find them healing themselves. It's easy to see that though bodily pain swiftly dissipates, the pain of memory remains, and so he paints his face with a shadowy smile and decides to try to physically destroy the ghouls in his memory, the men who attacked him and Shelly.

There seems to be no period of mediation between the birth of a feeling within him and its subsequent appearance on and through his body. It's all organic, as Brandon Lee described. Eric is unselfconscious, all spirit without the logical or rational trying to keep his emotions in check. While Eric is certainly in costume as a joker to reflect his inner torment (like a teenager wearing all black because *it's not a phase, Mom*), there is no additional artifice about him, no desire to manipulate or subjugate the way that others, like his murderers, do.

In the comic, a couple of the gang members stand in awe of Eric as he kills everyone around them; they, like the reader, can see the purity of his pain and the lengths he's willing to go to for love. Eric's foes stand ashamed, almost intuitively understanding that they have earned their demise. In the book, O'Barr has Fun Boy accept and even welcome his death, asking Eric for advice for the afterlife, knowing he has brought on his own perdition. In the film, only T-Bird is brought to this sublime awe, and, realizing the pain he has caused Eric, T-Bird weeps in a daze, repeating to himself that singular line from John Milton's *Paradise Lost*: "abashed the devil stood and felt how awful goodness is," which he had mockingly spat at Shelly before raping her, insulting her love of reading poetry, ridiculing it as feminine in the context of an extreme and violent assertion of toxic masculinity. This time, though, he understands the weight of these beautiful words.[105]

If toxic masculinity has a man stoically masking his feelings, then a soft masculinity contains the freedom to feel physically, spreading cerebral, spirited feelings (bad or good) throughout the body and honoring them. And by extension, that freedom to feel extends to the audience, who might have emotions of their own that Eric would most certainly never judge. He frustrates traditional notions of the way a man ought to behave in the

---

[105] John Milton, *Paradise Lost* (Penguin Classics, 2000).

way that Kurt Cobain, uncaring of societal notions, did with his clothes, carrying his complex feelings about gender literally on his sleeve. For Eric, it's not just his dark costume and makeup that mark him as uniquely different, it's also his physical freedom to behave the way he feels.

What is guiding Eric through the violence in this film isn't something rational, not some reasoning as watertight as a mathematical equation; rather, it's something as old as the Code of Hammurabi: revenge.[106] Eric is guided by something as passionate and simple as an eye for an eye, something Western societies have outlawed.

Brandon Lee leans so deeply into Eric that even how Eric fights is often intentionally sloppy. Recall Lee's training as an actor — taught the method, he would have understood that a musician like Eric does not have a martial arts background. Accordingly, to watch Eric fight is to watch a man trip and stumble, grimace, and leer as he hurts bad guys and is hurt in turn but isn't daunted. Eric lacks the control that Jake Lo in *Rapid Fire* possesses in his martial arts, even as he is stunned by his situation. Jake Lo has the steadiness of training guiding his surprised moves: he very obviously sticks to what he has learned, always snapping to correct form, often to a fault, only growing flexible as he understands what it means to apply learned technique to the irregularities of the real world.

---

106 Believed to have been written by Babylonian king Hammurabi in the ancient Near East sometime between 1755 and 1750 BC, the Code of Hammurabi is one of our earliest and best-preserved legal texts. One of its laws gives us the principle of exact reciprocity, or an eye for an eye.

Eric, on the other hand, begins from a place of spontaneity and has no correct stance that he returns to after dealing a blow. He has an erratic style more akin to street fighting, often falling into and with his adversaries as he lands a punch. Never once does Lee have Eric snap to a basic stance; his combat varies from circumstance to circumstance, his moves manifesting in response to his jogged memories and how much hate and anger is stirred within him. He makes greater use of his environment in a slapdash sort of way, often wielding his enemies' tools against them. Sometimes he bitch-slaps them, but most of the time he is guided by his feelings, rushing to pummel the bad guys headfirst, literally. Compared to the steady and poised Jake Lo, Eric Draven is a careening tornado, uncontrolled and very dangerous.

\*

All of Eric's selfish and avenging violence in the film would not be possible without the purest, most devoted, gutting kind of love, the kind James O'Barr felt and wrote into Eric, the kind so beautiful one might be lucky to experience at all. It's the kind of love that gives Eric tunnel vision, making it so that he forgets himself completely. Eric, in film and comic, would not be as nihilistically violent without the ability to love in the strongest, most self-abnegating way possible. It's a kind of love that once experienced, never leaves the body, a kind that once lost, saps a life of meaning. Even in death, Eric is capable of loving desperately and maniacally, as demonstrated not just through Shelly, but also in the bonds he comes to form with Albrecht and Sarah.

After killing Fun Boy, Eric visits Albrecht at his home to try and understand the specifics of what happened to him and Shelly. Eric appears, yelling "Freeze," and scares Albrecht nearly to death. It's one of the film's greatest scenes. The energetic and kinetic Lee, towering at six feet tall, manages to look as small and confused and scared as a child while he learns how Albrecht tried his best to apprehend those responsible for the murders.

When Eric says, "I don't know what I am," in response to Albrecht's question of whether he is a ghost, his mood shifts, and he becomes warm and vulnerable. He is not entirely clear on what kind of an entity he is, metaphysically, even if he said he might be a clown when talking to Sarah.

This scene in Albrecht's home is as comforting as a warm fire on a blistering day to me and to Eric, too. Unlike the cool, rational, manly man, he asks Albrecht for help and talks in an effort to better understand the world and his new role in it. In one of the film's sequels — *Salvation* — the version of Eric portrayed is so close to a traditionally masculine man that it's a part of the franchise only in name. Actor Eric Mabius created an Eric character (here named Alex) who is calculating, collecting, and works on his own to investigate. He makes up his mind and plans out his attacks in such a glaring contrast to Brandon Lee's Eric, who tearfully begs everyone for information and demands they remember what they did to him.

In this scene, the lens looks at Lee steadily, placing the whole of him in frame. He has his arms crossed, and he looks hunched and small. He's looking around the place slowly. It's yellow and welcoming, like his own had been, marigold. After a pause that isn't so much meditative as hopelessly tired, Eric looks up at Albrecht. His eyebrows raise in the way I raise mine sometimes to keep myself from weeping.

"I thought I'd use your front door," he says in response to Albrecht's question as to whether he will magically disappear. He replies in the way a regular mortal person would and shows that, at his core, he's just one man to whom something terrible has happened, even though this "something terrible" has ruined his entire world. "I'm sorry as hell for what happened to you and your girlfriend," Albrecht says, but it isn't an apology for him to make.

Eric trembles ever so slightly, as if silent sobs are wracking through him. "Yeah," he whispers. Tears pool in his eyes but don't spill, and he walks out. Brandon Lee's grace here is heartbreaking but also spellbinding; he carries Eric with gravitas but also levity, never hamming it up or bungling the delivery. He is pitch-perfect with his comedic timing and emotional beats. In this scene with Albrecht, Lee gives us Eric unmasked, molten and, full-bodied, what he might have been like in moments of calm during his short life; he gives us the vulnerability, the humanity, that allows the eternal sidekick of The Fool to so successfully be a protagonist or, in other words, the true King at last.

✽

In chasing his final mark, Skank (Angel David), Eric wanders into one of Top Dollar's meetings, a kind of sabbath gathering of goons, where Skank has taken refuge. Eric interrupts Top Dollar's rant about Devil's Night to say he doesn't care about any of them, he is just there to collect and punish Skank. In the ensuing violence, Eric only ends up killing them all because they won't let him leave with Skank. This scene perfectly embodies Niko Stratis's point about Cobain: Eric isn't angry at Top Dollar, who personifies the system, for he doesn't know yet that Top ordered that he and Shelly be disposed of.

The film paints an intriguing contrast between Eric and Top Dollar. The latter is cool as a cowboy. But he is also charming and cracks jokes in the midst of battle in the way Eric does. What sets the two apart is Top Dollar's steeliness, his ability to turn off his sadness at the drop of a hat, or the joy he takes in violence for violence's sake. In the film's final moments, Top tells Eric that the order he gave to have him and Shelly killed was nothing personal. It was just business, an act to clear their apartment, Top's macabre form of bureaucracy. This impersonality is what differentiates him from Eric.

Because the thing is Eric possesses an indelible and integral goodness, a humanity that is apparent in him before he becomes *The* Crow. Eric was always a fool for love. In one of his flashbacks to his previous life, we see Eric in Shelly's arms, asking her to tell him again and again that she loves him, just to repeat the phrase over and over. A dopey smile spreads across his face as he closes his eyes in a blissful sleep. We also know Eric was good in life through Sarah, who remembers his kindness. Eric never hurts anyone who doesn't deserve it, and he never cares to hurt anyone who didn't hurt him. He is reborn with his moral sensibility intact, as well as his desire for love. He's kind and gentle toward Gabriel, feeding him, petting him with a tender caress. This is a good man, warm with passions, unlike the cold and rational Top Dollar, who conceals his feelings and plays mind games with everyone around him.

There is a scene in the film that I've always had a bit of trouble with, a little vignette that comes before the film's final beats. Eric has killed his final mark, Skank, and is walking back to the cemetery with The Crow astride his shoulder, his mission complete. He is tired and takes a moment to lean against a beam. Flashlights shine in his face; they belong to a gaggle of kids out trick-or-treating, and they run toward him in merriment and costume. As they pass by him, laughing and whooping, Eric joins them hungrily in full-bodied laughter, the first time he's laughed so breezily in a year. It's a scene that was tough for me because I didn't understand it, and I used to think it was a bit cheesy. But now I think it's beautiful — Eric's soul, after a year, has found calm, and though he has been laughing throughout the film (maniacally, tauntingly), this is the first time the laughter stems from genuine mirth. He's accomplished his mission, and now he can be with Shelly again.

Immediately after this optimistic scene, Eric is back at the cemetery and has a conversation with a weeping Sarah. Throughout the film, Eric runs into the child as she skateboards through the decrepit and grimy city. Before the film's explosive denouement, Sarah is sleeping on Shelly's grave, next to Eric's plot. Eric nudges her awake. He sits cross-legged before her. His frame, which earlier loomed and towered as it doled out punches and threw blades, seems so small again, like in Albrecht's apartment, as small as Sarah's frail, emaciated frame, small in the way Kurt Cobain often looked as though swimming in his mossy cardigans. (It is this scene that, after watching it, The Boy was forced to acknowledge Lee's deftness in playing vulnerability.) Sarah is weeping — Shelly, and by extension Eric, offered her the only kindness she ever received in her life. When she tells Eric that he left her without saying goodbye, that he died without saying goodbye, Eric's eyebrows knit. Her words have speared him.

"You're just gonna have to forgive me for that," he says in a voice that is small and soft like a blanket but steady and blunt as a goodbye, as if straining to keep a wail in his throat. It's a voice so unlike the robust cackle that erupted from him before he killed Tin Tin, so unlike the screams that sounded like skin grating against gravel, even unlike his quiet and tired sadness at Albrecht's home. While earlier Eric's voice was febrile and volatile, wide and vibrating with wrath, here it falters and his tears can be heard in its tremble; he's hushed like he's talking through a mouthful of cotton balls. This scene never fails to move me because of the closure it offers that, though full of love, still lands like a blow to the gut.

The line doesn't carry any profound knowledge and, in less capable hands, could have been conveyed flatly. Lee's delivery endows the phrase with the heft of a salutary verse; he turns the phrase into an honest truth that he knows to be prickly, for Shelly left him without saying goodbye, too. Even though Eric has killed every bad soul who hurt him, he is still faced with his own guilt about his and Shelly's deaths, which this child has him finally countenance: "And you're never coming back," Sarah says. Eric doesn't know what to say, so he smiles a sad smile and gives Sarah Shelly's engagement ring. When Sarah hugs him with tears streaming down her face, Eric trembles — he can still feel others' pain through touch. We don't get a vignette this time, only Eric's shudder. Eric's breathing is shallow; he is so deeply affected by the departure, but he withstands it this time and doesn't rail against it.

Acceptance, finally.

Moments later, we see him place flowers on Shelly's grave. It's a simple and sparse scene, but coming after Sarah, it is instructive. Sarah gets him to realize and vocalize that sometimes forgiveness is the only thing possible after death, the only response to the death of a loved one. After the violence of revenge, Eric finally has time to act out forgiveness, move through the process of grieving, which The Crow worked to actuate. He is forgiving Shelly for leaving, and he is forgiving himself for not preventing her death and his own death and for the pain it has caused Sarah. After doling out revenge, Eric is finally ready to touch and gift tokens of forgiveness. It's an act that is beautiful, and it feels as heavy as shooting a horse in the head.

## INTERLUDE II

A memory I often replay in my mind is one that also hurts me to remember.

In the same breath as my mind enlivens it, it also cautions me against it, like The Crow trying to pull Eric out of his own sad, sweet reveries. It's a memory from that first summer. It's the afternoon again, and we're sharing a bottle of red wine on the little balcony of his East End apartment, right above a Vietnamese restaurant. We are just talking. He brings out his acoustic guitar (I learn later that he needs something to do with his hands, that he can't keep them idle — it helps him to think, to focus) and begins strumming a song he's only been able to wrangle the first few notes of. I start talking about myself, something I'm not very good at doing for lack of practice. I talk about my past and it's sad. As I get deeper into my sadness, arriving at the depressing core of my story, his hands fall still, with one falling flat on the fretboard to silence the strings. He looks at me and just listens as I talk. It is an open sort of listening, with a visible respect for my words. I have never, at that point in my life, experienced that kind of still reception before, at least not from a man.

I haven't experienced it often since him, either.

The other day, I tried to write a letter from his perspective. I wanted an apology for how he used me, and if I couldn't get a real one, I could try to craft one. But as I tried to write, I couldn't think of anything he would say because I don't think he has ever felt sorry. I did end up writing a couple of lines, but they sounded more like something I would say to myself. "I am sorry for hurting you," I ended. And then, a few lines down, in my own voice, I wrote, "It's okay." This moment of forgiveness is not something I can guarantee I will believe when I get sad and self-destructive, but because I wrote it and felt it, I can hold it up to myself like a photograph, like evidence.

It's tough to be logical when one is in so, so, so much pain when you're pressing on the same bruise again and again and keeping it from healing. I have a hard time with hope because so much of it is forward-looking, and I am so often trapped in my mind. I have a hard time with hope because it's difficult work involving self-awareness and accountability, things that seem impossible to access when the wound is fresh. But now that I have acted out self-forgiveness, it's in my past, and it's a memory that I can also turn to, maybe.

*You're just gonna have to forgive me for that*, I can remind myself.

# 4

**Continued Breath**

Brandon Lee bemoaned the idea of sequels for *The Crow*. "It's a very self-contained story," he says in the on-set interview excerpted from a much longer 90-minute interview collecting dust on a producer's shelf.[107] He's in between shots and maintains a level of professionalism as an interviewee, but he is also balancing his character, who he will have to jump into at any minute. Even so, his charisma and sense of humor come through in delicious bursts. He seems tired and cold. He's in Eric's dark costume, under which he wears a bulletproof vest — his hair falls across his face, it's dry and apparently not yet wetted by the world's rain, and he's chain-smoking

---

[107] "The Crow Brandon Lee on Set Interview Rare 1993," November 13, 2022, https://www.youtube.com/watch?v=ke75Cab4I7o.

cigarettes. "Once it's over," he shrugs and trails off for a split second. "I mean, I haven't even begun to think about what *Crow 18* would be. I just hope we shoot it someplace warmer," he says with a childlike smile.

Because the film is now a cult classic, because it has a devoted following, the brutal machine of Hollywood tries again and again to launch sequels and remakes in an effort to cash in on what it sees as a ready-made audience. But machines have neither soul nor heart, and all of *The Crow*'s remakes always scan to me as redundant, ruthlessly vivifying, and dry attempts that are morally, spiritually, emotionally, and even epistemically bankrupt. Each one of the three standalone sequels — 1996's *City of Angels*, 2000's *Salvation*, and 2005's *Wicked Prayer* — is a paint-by-numbers rehash of the 1994 film, as opposed to being a work inspired by the original film's soul. Major plot points are replicated — a couple's brutal murder, the man's rebirth, his crow companion, revenge, and final rest — but in slightly varying dress. Each sequel feebly attempts to differentiate itself from the original, and in doing so, it ends up having only style and regurgitated substance (*City of Angels*) or an incomprehensible and needlessly complex story (*Salvation*) that leaves the central character sidelined in his own tale (*Wicked Prayer*). Ultimately, though, as each sequel strives to deliver the original's impact, it is left feeling faded, like a photocopy or a poor transliteration.

Each of the subsequent actors' work mines Lee's dynamic character for their plot's requirements, ultimately projecting onto the screen an exaggerated part of Lee's doomed hero to hollow effect without adding anything distinct of their own. Vincent Pérez in *City of Angels* gives us the tragic, quixotic romantic without any sense of humor; he's almost pathetic as he wails without poetic grace. Eric Mabius in *Salvation* offers us only the vengeful figure, leaving us with a calculating and cold figure like Top Dollar. And Edward Furlong in *Wicked Prayer* gives us the comical Crow that is pure Fool, feebly gesturing toward the charm that Lee naturally had. Lee is the only one who is able to offer us dynamic humanity — a man aching, tender, angry, kind, complex, and hoping for salvation in hopeless circumstances. Lee offers an Eric with human beats, changeable and fluid.

The visceral life Lee breathed into *The Crow* — that timeless ache that reaches back in time to Poe and those souls who wept from grief before him, to forward in time to me and others like me — created an eternal soul that is carried better in a film that seemingly has nothing to do with Eric Draven. Perhaps no other piece of art encapsulates *The Crow*'s bleeding, beating heart as specifically and precisely as 2014's *John Wick*. *John Wick* is, like all good translations, as much a work of art unto itself as it is *The Crow*'s spiritual kin, carrying literal meaning with different, yet still lyrical, words.

*John Wick* does carry a few direct connections with *The Crow*. Its director, Chad Stahelski, was taught by Brandon Lee's martial arts teacher and stepped in after Lee's death to serve as a double on the set of *The Crow*. Furthermore, the two films share the same motif of memory and photographs and feature both a quixotic love for a woman with a literary name and a reemergence from the grave. Even actor David Patrick Kelly (T-Bird) makes an appearance. Much of *John Wick*'s iconography recalls *The Crow*, too, specifically its folkloric bent. John is called Baba Yaga and is feared as a monster would be feared. But he is also described as so fearsome that he is Baba Yaga's hunter. Eric, likewise, is called The Crow, even as he is being shepherded by The Crow, while he also embodies theater's Fool archetype. But what makes the film its own unique and marvelous entity is John Wick himself or Keanu Reeves's characterization of him.

Where Lee's Eric is flamboyant and erratic, embodying a loud and soft, feminine masculinity, dancing and cracking jokes and quoting Gothic poetry, Reeves's Wick is demure, still, and pensive. Ostensibly, John Wick is very much the picture of traditional masculinity — not saying much, John is pure action, pure will directed at a goal, calculating and seemingly mechanical. But I would say that there's something else, something riotous and molten, going on here, with Reeves's portrayal and with the story itself, something that carries *The Crow*'s bleeding heart.

The film's plot is very simple. John Wick is a hit man who comes out of retirement after his puppy is killed and his car is stolen to punish those responsible. John is enraged because the puppy was a gift from his wife, Helen, who passed away from cancer mere days earlier. Like *The Crow*, this film is impossibly cool, casting Reeves as an assassin who, unflinching and uttering very few words, effectively achieves his goal. Though flamboyance isn't John's style, he is still, in his own Reevesian way, very emotional. Much like Kurt Cobain and Eric Draven, all John wants to do in this movie is feel in isolation: he wants to process grief and he wants hope (in the form of a puppy), and when an annoying brat gets in his way, all he wants is revenge. Like Cobain and Eric, all John does is geared toward or in service to making himself feel better.

Very early on in the film, Viggo (Michael Nyqvist), head of New York's Russian mafia and father of Iosef (Alfie Allen), the young man who kills John's puppy and steals his car, calls John. John is in his basement, excavating his old life in a scene much like Eric Draven crawling out of his grave. In the way that Eric bursts through wet earth and is reborn in *The Crow*, John spearheads his own rebirth by cracking into the ground and digging up his weapons and clothes from his assassin days, which had been cast in concrete in his basement. "Let us not resort to our baser instincts and handle this like civilized men," Viggo says with calculated calm in a desperate attempt to save his son. Viggo knows very well that John intends and will succeed in killing Iosef. Without uttering a single word, grunt, or breath, John hangs up. He will not be civilized.

Later, at the Hotel Continental's bar, John sees Addy (Bridget Regan), a bartender he knew in his working days. "I've never seen you like this," Addy says to John. "Like what?" he asks, puzzled. "Vulnerable," Addy says. Indeed, John has been moving slowly, as though sodden with tears, and his silence seems to express irritation at not being allowed the space, time, and solitude to think only of Helen. In addressing Addy, a soft smile buds on John's face that's more than courtesy, that says that Addy is a friend, but it doesn't bloom big — and we know it can bloom big because we see him beam during his memories of Helen. It's as if he isn't yet ready to feel the happiness carried in a wider grin. Reeves has always excelled at massaging depth — pain, sadness, anger, love — into a character's contours while maintaining a heavy stillness, understanding his characters' limits. Just as Eric only shows us what he feels, John, a less irreverent and impassioned personality, also shows us what he feels.

He moves in clean lines and swiftly, which seems to be necessitated to keep sobs from wracking through his body. Reeves conveys his character's humanity through a bracketed, hushed screen presence, a deft understanding of his form and the body's ability to delicately convey nuanced feelings, like the inability to smile too broadly, at least not yet. John isn't a robot, Reeves shows, and this isn't a movie about mindless slaughter. Through subtleties that are buttressed and punctuated by explosions of white-hot anger, Reeves allows John to emerge as a man honoring his feelings, wanting mightily to process his grief.

In a scene that is a direct corollary to the one in *The Crow*, where Eric walks into Top Dollar's board meeting asking for Skank, John confronts Viggo and says to him, "Step aside. Give me your son." Like Eric, John doesn't care to make a point about how mafiosos are running amok in his world; he doesn't care to fix the system that birthed an entitled, violent man like Iosef. So much of this film is ambient, consequential anger, and Iosef and Viggo are mere hurdles in John's life as he works to find steady emotional ground, but once present, they become channels for the processing of his anger and sadness.

When Viggo asks John why he won't just let his son go and says his loss was a mere dog and car, we see John deliver us the reasoning behind his madness that Reeves has already conveyed to us through his tears, his clutching of Helen's bracelet, and his endless watching of a video he filmed of Helen before her death.

John says that when he received the puppy the night of Helen's funeral, he found hope. "In that moment, I received some semblance of hope, an opportunity to grieve unalone," John says. "And your son took that from me. Stole that from me. Killed that from me. People keep asking me if I'm back, and I haven't really had an answer. But now, yeah, I'm thinking I'm back. So you can either hand over your son. Or you can die screaming alongside him." John veritably growls the latter half of his short speech, and when he says, "took that from me," he sounds like a feral monster. It is the most terrifying Reeves has been on screen, his already deep voice becoming hellish, like a blade against brimstone.

This confession — fired at Viggo not so much like daggers but like hellfire, coming from the roiling anger within John's belly, from that spirited place, as Plato might call it, of anger and unprocessed grief — speaks to John's intense sadness and fear and ire and loneliness. All this speaks to everything messy and passionate churning within him unresolved, everything that traditional masculinity might require a man never to show to others. John's confession is aching, honest, and allowed to burst forth from him in desperation. It's emotional and turbulent and unhinged, everything that the traditionally masculine man is not, at least not publicly.

"Do I look civilized to you?" John fires at the film's end as he kills Viggo, a kind of belated answer to Viggo's earlier plea for civility and rational behavior. The rampage that this film charts is John's attempt to rebuild hope after a world-shattering loss followed swiftly by another loss. Later films ask John when his rampages, inspired by various motives for revenge, will stop. I think John would know that revenge doesn't solve anything, that it will not magically bring Helen back. But it is action after all, and to anyone who has been so profoundly hopeless as John feels in this first film, John's actions scan as meaningful because they are inspired by the intuitive knowledge that even irrational actions are better than nothing. For why else would he ceremoniously unearth his old assassin's costume? He is Poe's narrator, rejoicing at the raven's appearance when Viggo calls. Even if, ultimately, John's revenge is futile, even if it is mere thrashing in an uncaring world, it helps him feel better for the moment about the dog and by extension Helen, for through its enactment, it honors his feelings of anger, indignation, and lack of control.

John sustains a wound early on in the film as he hunts for Iosef. It's on his abdomen, doled out by a henchman who drives a broken champagne bottle into his gut. Throughout the film, various adversaries repeatedly hit John in that wound so as to debilitate and momentarily overpower him. But at the film's end, in a battle against Viggo, John uses his wound to his advantage. Viggo has a knife poised before John's stomach, and John pulls at Viggo's hand and knife, stabbing himself. Viggo is taken by surprise, and John uses this to overpower him.

He pulls the knife out of himself and thrusts it into Viggo. It's a totally insane move, and as he scowls from his pain, John looks terrifying and beastly. His expression is the same monstrous lunacy as Eric's maniacal laughter in Fun Boy's face as the bullet hole in his hand heals, as the leer he wears at Gideon's pawn shop after Gideon shoots him and before he lunges like a wildcat. If a man welcomes this kind of pain and smirks in its face, then imagine how terrible the emotional pain must be that makes him weep.

John's leveraging of his own pain to overpower Viggo is also redolent of how *The Crow* ends when Eric defeats Top Dollar. "I have something to give you," Eric says. "I don't want it anymore." If Eric can feel others' pain through touch, then surely he can transfer it to other people, too. And this is exactly what he does. Eric overpowers Top by giving him "thirty hours of pain, all at once, all for you." The pain immobilizes and debilitates Top, and Eric, weeping, pushes him off the roof. This is what John does, too: he stabs himself and then takes that same knife and thrusts it into Viggo, depositing his hurt into Viggo, as if to show him how he feels, how he has been made to feel. Both these films end on a plea of sorts, asking us to feel their protagonists' pain, to carry it.

*John Wick*'s final moments present us with a tender vignette, but even so, it reveals something desperate and hungry in John. The toll a lack of a healthy grieving process takes on a person becomes most evident in this scene. John stumbles into a dog shelter, and as he staples the wound on his abdomen, he notices a pit bull marked to be put down. He staggers over to the sweet dog. In a voraciously hungry way, John reaches for and guides the dog out of his cage. "C'mon, let's go home," he says, and the dog trails after him.

It's heartbreaking, this grasping for some semblance of Helen at all, and in this scene, this denouement, Reeves stunningly portrays in his mesmerizingly still way a kind of clawing desperation in John Wick, how terribly he needs hope, how the only way he can now get hope is to build it for himself. He hasn't yet found the need to forgive himself for his survivor's guilt. Though this end certainly portends a kind of healing for John, there's something about it that makes me immensely sad. It depicts what Niko Stratis writes about Kurt Cobain: it's a frustrated attempt to seek control over his own situation. Having lost Helen and the puppy irrevocably, he gets another dog, any dog at all, to bring him back to the moment of first receiving the puppy and hearing Helen's voice in the accompanying note. He seems caught in Poe's "The Raven," looking for another distraction, not having yet learned that he's just going to have to forgive Helen for dying.

*John Wick* was and remains immensely popular, and I think one of the reasons it found such a large audience was what many faulted *The Crow* for: a logically sparse plot, which is really profoundly emotionally rich, containing a grungy beating, dark heart. I think *John Wick*'s tragedy is that there are sequels. Don't get me wrong, they are great fun, but all the man wants is to be left alone. Present-day Hollywood loves sequels and franchises because they guarantee profit. John Wick's universe is now becoming a multiverse, with spin-offs and crossovers on the horizon. I don't think that this is the way to keep the bleeding heart alive.

"The comic book is an underground comic book," Lee says about *The Crow* in the film's featurette. "It's not Spider-Man or Superman, it's not something for mass consumption, and it has a very hard edge to it." It is this hard edge that is also its personality, its emotional core, which becomes calcified the more it is reproduced, in the way that an image is lost and sapped of meaning the more it is photocopied. *John Wick* wasn't a photocopy of *The Crow*, it was a translation for modern-day audiences, carrying the original's soul but also its own, marrying them in an entirely different manner and carriage. It wasn't trying to be like *The Crow* at all, carrying its own interpretation of the original story's broad strokes and turns, which is what allowed for Lee's legacy to remain alive.

\*

"Brandon Lee was a friend, and I'd never do anything to hurt his legacy," O'Barr said in 2014 when he was still a part of the production process of a remake that had cast Luke Evans as Eric.[108] O'Barr was asked by the interviewer to assuage fans' fears, specifically those who believed that no one ought to reprise Lee's role. "I'd also remind them that Eric Draven was a creation of the movie — if you read the comic, Eric and

---

108 Sean C.W. Korsgaard, "Interview with James O'Barr, Creator of The Crow," *Korsgaard's Commentary*, March 4, 2015, archived March 8, 2016, https://web.archive.org/web/20160308133633/http://www.korsgaardscommentary.com/2014/10/interview-james-obarr-creator-crow.html.

Shelley [*sic*] never have their last names revealed. Hopefully, this is one area the new movie being more faithful to the comic will come into play, and Eric won't be going by Eric Draven in the new film. Luke Evens [*sic*] may play Eric, but Brandon Lee will forever be Eric Draven."[109]

In the summer of 2024, director Rupert Sanders offered us his adaptation of O'Barr's graphic novel. A reboot of *The Crow* film series had been in the works since 2008, with various directors and actors linked to the project. O'Barr gave his blessing to a reinterpretation after director F. Javier Gutiérrez visited him in 2014. Gutiérrez was slated to direct with Evans as lead.

"He got off the airplane, I took him to my car, and I was going to lecture him for an hour and then put him right back on the plane," O'Barr said in 2014.[110] He explained to the director that "no one wants this, no one wants to see a remake, that the original is sacred ground because it was Brandon Lee's last film, that you're committing career suicide by trying to remake that film."[111] But he soon changed his mind when Gutiérrez assured him that he didn't so much want to helm a remake of the 1994 film as he wanted to adapt his graphic novel page for page.[112]

But over the course of a decade, things shifted: both Gutiérrez and Evans went on to pursue projects with conflicting schedules. Eventually, Rupert Sanders, director of *Snow White*

---

109 Ibid.

110 Ibid.

111 Ibid.

112 Ibid.

*and the Huntsman* and *Ghost in the Shell*, was brought on with Bill Skarsgård as Eric Draven and FKA Twigs as Shelly Webster.

Though the 2024 film takes pains to let us know that it is a reinterpretation of O'Barr's work, crediting him for the story with pronounced flair in the opening credits, it makes equal, if not more diligent, reference to Proyas's film through Eric and Shelly's names, and the character of Kronos, who functions like Skull Cowboy was intended to. (In the graphic novel, The Crow debriefs Eric on certain supernatural matters. Proyas's film tried to sidestep the talking animal trope with Skull Cowboy, and when that didn't work out, Sarah quickly summarizes Eric's reason for being reborn.) What's more, characters seem to quote David Schow and John Shirley's script verbatim at points. Time and again in Sanders's film, Kronos says that Eric needs to go back to the realm of the living to "put the wrong things right," echoing Sarah's words, but nowhere are Schow and Shirley credited for the words they forged after Brandon Lee's death.

Here, Eric and Shelly seem not so much as viscerally linked soulmates as they do two people who have just met and are figuring each other out because that's what they are. Sanders and screenwriters Zach Baylin and William Schneider have Eric and Shelly meet after Shelly has already come into contact with the film's confusing bad guy, played by Danny Huston. Skarsgård's Eric registers the prematurity of the label of love on his and Shelly's relationship when, in death, he begins to experience doubt about Shelly. After seeing footage of her committing murder, he wonders about the person he thought he fell in love with. In conversation with Kronos, who explains how this hole in their love impacts Eric's immortality, Eric offers to trade his soul for Shelly's — he tells Kronos that, after revenge, he will willingly go to the afterlife if Shelly is brought back to life. Kronos agrees, and Eric goes back to his mission.

If Eric chooses to trade his soul, this means that he and Shelly will never be together again; such an inevitability would be unthinkable for the Eric in James O'Barr's novel or the Eric played by Brandon Lee, for someone who saw the person they loved as their reason for being. Eric, as personified by Skarsgård, doesn't seem to care about . . . much. We don't see any pain or sadness in this film; we are only told that it should be there.

This film's emotional bankruptcy is best displayed in its feeble rendition of "Sparklehorse." Sanders begins his film with an image of a white horse wrapped in barbed wire, which young Eric watches mournfully. The horse dies, but when Eric's soul is traded for Shelly's, the horse is brought back to life. With elementary understanding; the film seems to know that Sparklehorse contains a meaningful metaphor, but it doesn't understand exactly what it represents. The horse could potentially represent love or hope, but only in a soulless, futile way, for Shelly and Eric will forever be separated, each left to sleepily mourn their loss against a fate that they cannot fight anymore.

When Skarsgård's Eric is shot after he experiences doubt about Shelly, the bullet strikes him in the abdomen. Sanders lingers over Skarsgård with a medium shot as Eric lies there bleeding out. When Eric returns to life moments later, that wound in his abdomen heals dramatically on frame. The mechanics of this scene — in the face of what happened to Lee, in the face of the fact that this film is toying around with Proyas's film and Lee's version of Eric Draven — seem a revisionist "correction" of Lee's passing, an attempt at putting the wrong thing right, when really it feels like an unimaginative filmmaker using a real-life tragedy and its trauma as superficial, cinematic fodder. And for this reason, Sanders's film is just another instance of IP mining and a Hollywood production that only postures as and mimics art — exploitive and unforgivable. It fulfills O'Barr's worst fear of trampling on the "sacred ground" of Brandon Lee's final performance.

\*

Philosopher and cultural critic Walter Benjamin wrote what has now become a foundational and eerily prescient piece in 1935 called "The Work of Art in the Age of Mechanical Reproduction." In it, Benjamin talks about how modernity and industrialization birthed a new mode by which to reproduce works of art. While in the past, the original work of art held authority over its manual reproduction (a forgery, for example, of an original painting), in contemporary times, mechanical reproduction (such as a photograph of a landscape or a vinyl recording of a live choral performance) exists independently of the original and with as much credibility and authority.

What's more, mechanical reproduction always depreciates the quality of the original artwork. According to Benjamin, the original work of art contains an authenticity, which is its "essence," that distinct and contextualized aspect about the artwork (all the space and time that informs its existence) that is communicated to the viewer, themselves existing within a historical moment. An original work of art is something human communicated to us as earthly people. Mechanical reproductions, on the other hand, exist in a manner that isn't linked to history. They, removed from time and space like the Cartesian mind, are out of conversation with the artwork they are reproducing, and as such, reproductions do not have authenticity or an aura. For Benjamin, they lack a soul.

*The Crow* and Lee's effort and presence within it constitute a unique existence, all within an original work of art that didn't reproduce O'Barr's own artwork. It translated it — the humanity within O'Barr's work spoke to Proyas and Lee, who then added something of themselves, of their humanity, to *The Crow*. In the way that *John Wick* carries *The Crow*'s soul, so too does the film carry O'Barr's graphic novel's soul. While it certainly could be said that *The Crow*'s producers banked on making money with the film, they were, at least by proximity to artists Proyas and Lee, also working toward creating a work of art.

All the sequels have been mechanical reproductions aspiring for the original's authenticity, but they have never achieved it. The sequels work to replicate Proyas's film instead of focusing on creating something resonant or with its own identity in space and time. And if the proliferation of bland and formulaic superhero movies, produced by a conservative system so hungry for profit it relegates genuine art to the sidelines, is anything to go by, any further remakes of *The Crow* will dishonor the artistic magic that sparked between O'Barr's and Proyas's film, the authentic trade of an understanding of pain and love. Even Top Dollar, when talking to his henchmen about the need to abandon Devil's Night because it has become a common greeting-card holiday and has therefore lost its edge, notes that an idea, once it becomes a predictable institution, is not worth backing.

The latest remake — in whose production, to the best of my knowledge, O'Barr played no role other than receiving a story credit — is a photocopy, which has a knack for killing and dulling that which is living and vibrant. More than anything, though, it could not contain the life that Brandon Lee infused into the 1994 film, and it certainly could not carry its breath and grieving legacy in the way *John Wick* does. It's nothing more than a slickly produced forgery with a gaping hole where a paper heart might fit.

## Conclusion

In June 2023, exactly a year after I first watched *The Crow* — a year that saw me turning to the film at any and every moment of sadness — my psychiatrist lessened my antidepressant dosage. Something within me clicked into place, and my emotions have since come to be so regulated. I often find myself yearning for a breakdown, for something other than stasis. *The Crow* has taken on a new function in my life. Where it worked before to remind me of a certain person I once loved, now, having found myself dealing with my past in a rather rational way, I turn to the film to be reminded of not another but myself. The film is a mirror into the tender bruise, the bleeding heart I used to be, and I find myself cherishing that aspect of myself that I often thought to be insane. Roger Ebert said he was grateful that *The Crow*'s producers released it despite its literal tragedy. I am grateful, too.

The past year has been the longest stretch of time that I have been stable mentally — the longest period of time since I was 15 years old. I haven't cried much, but that's because I haven't felt like crying much. I'm able to sit still through films, I'm able to laugh at my mistakes, I'm able to recognize negative thoughts before they spiral into catastrophe. I haven't wanted to kill myself in a year. I've become obsessed with art — films, books, artists — in a way I used to be when I was a teen. But instead of celebrating, I've been terrified in a way that feels dull, blunt. I'm worried that I won't remember how bad it got, that I will take my past for granted. I'm worried I won't be able to feel what I have celebrated in this book — all the colors of feeling. I'm worried I am numb. But at least I am alive.

This year, my antidepressant dosage was lowered further.

I don't know what has happened to The Boy. I don't think about him as desperately as I used to. I have reclaimed *The Crow* fully for myself now; writing this book has been a great help. The idea that I made him hate me hurts me less and less as I come to find it easier and easier to forgive myself. And the more I forgive myself, the more I remember I *have* and I *can* forgive myself. Something I have learned is a lesson that is useless: time heals wounds. To say this to a person in the midst of heartbreak, to have said this to Eric after his resurrection, would have been futile for a reason I hope I have expressed in this book: emotional pain has very real heft. A broken heart hurts so terribly sometimes that any other pain at all would be a nice welcome. Time does heal pain, distance fogs memory, but until a point in time has been reached where the pain doesn't feel like a broken bone in a sharp draft, the pain has to be borne. I have spent so many nights weeping myself to sleep. If not over The Boy, then over something else, like ideas of my own failure, my uselessness, hopelessness.

Medication does help, and it has gotten me to a point where I can give myself little tasks, the completion of which paints hope on my horizon, something to work toward. I'm worried that I will reach a certain point with my medication when I will stop feeling completely. But as I rewatched *The Crow* again and again as I wrote this book, I found myself tearing up. That I feel moved to tears watching this film, after a while of not being able to cry, makes me happy — my feelings are not only a celebration of my life but also the life within this film, a life that continues to hum.

"No one ever really dies as long as they are loved," O'Barr says in the 2010 introduction to his book. I hope he would be okay if I added to this: No one ever really dies as long as they have loved.

This desire of mine — to live life — is something that occupies me so, and it's why I look for it, why I write about it when I do see it in others, why I'm writing this book. Eric is instructive to me, maybe he even emboldens me to possess a kind of fearlessness and conviction in my feelings of and within loneliness. Feeling is meaningful, and the variance of feeling, whether negative or positive, ought to be honored despite material circumstances. To amend the timeless adage: to have lived and felt at all is better than the slumber of indifference or numbness. Eric has taught me to take a remove from myself when I feel lonely and to feel a kind of pleasure in that moment of loneliness — because I am alive at all. Having seen moments of intense suicidal ideation in the past, any indication of life thriving and throbbing within me now is something I have started to cherish.

Thank you, Brandon Lee.

# *Sources

AFI Catalog of Feature Films. "Dragon: The Bruce Lee Story." n.d. https://catalog.afi.com/Film/59508-DRAGON--THE-BRUCE-LEE-STORY?cxt=filmography.

Anderson, Philip. "Interviews: James O'Barr – Author of The Crow." *KAOS2000 Magazine*, July 20, 2000. Archived March 23, 2016. https://web.archive.org/web/20160323220745/http:/kaos2000.net/interviews/jamesobarr/.

Ascher-Walsh, Rebecca. "How *The Crow* Flew." *Entertainment Weekly*, May 13, 1994. Archived March 14, 2022. https://archive.org/details/entertainment-weekly-222-1994-05-13-brandon-lee-his-last-interview/page/18/mode/1up?view=theater

Benjamin, Walter. "The Work of Art in the Age of Mechanical Reproduction." Edited by Hannah Arendt. Translated by Harry Zohn. *Illuminations*. Schocken Books, 1969. https://web.mit.edu/allanmc/www/benjamin.pdf.

Berardinelli, James. "Review: The Crow." *Reelviews*, 1994. https://preview.reelviews.net/movies/c/crow.html.

Bird, Simon. "The Crow: The Graphic Novel." Thecrow.info, 1998. Archived September 16, 2016. https://web.archive.org/web/20160916202142/http:/www.thecrow.info/granovel.htm.

Blu-ray Extras. "Introducing: Brandon Lee – The Action Hero of the 90's." YouTube, December 22, 2018. https://www.youtube.com/watch?v=IXaTzOz5HRs.

Biography.com. "Brandon Lee Biography." February 22, 2024. https://www.biography.com/actors/brandon-lee.

The Bobbie Wygant Archive. "Brandon Lee 'Rapid Fire' 7/13/92 - Bobbie Wygant Archive." YouTube, November 7, 2020. https://www.youtube.com/watch?v=u_xX8yw_arY.

Bordo, Susan. *The Flight to Objectivity: Essays on Cartesianism and Culture*. SUNY Press, 1987.

Box Office Mojo. "Batman." n.d. https://www.boxofficemojo.com/title/tt0096895/.

Brandon LeeMovement. "Michael Massee on Extra: Talks About Brandon Lee Shooting." YouTube, April 2, 2007. https://www.youtube.com/watch?v=Zjn3WqsvE_Q.

Business, Catch, and Elle Nash, eds. *Witch Craft Magazine*. Print. Vol. 5, 2019.

Caliber Comics. "About Us," n.d. https://calibercomics.com/about-us.

Clover, Carol J. *Men, Women, and Chain Saws: Gender in the Modern Horror Film*. Princeton University Press, 1992.

Coste, Françoise. "'Women, Ladies, Girls, Gals…': Ronald Reagan and the Evolution of Gender Roles in the United States." *Miranda*, no. 12 (February 24, 2016). https://doi.org/10.4000/miranda.8602.

Cotter, Padraig. "*The Crow* Movie: The Deleted Skull Cowboy Explained." *ScreenRant*, June 21, 2019. https://screenrant.com/crow-movie-skull-cowboy-deleted-subplot-explained/.

CS Carson. "Brandon Lee with Jim Whaley on Cinema Showcase." YouTube, December 4, 2022. https://www.youtube.com/watch?v=J2fNBIj6opM.

Ebert, Roger. "Reviews: The Crow." RogerEbert.com, May 13, 1994. https://www.rogerebert.com/reviews/the-crow-1994.

Faludi, Susan. *Backlash: The Undeclared War Against American Women*. Crown, 2006.

Flackett, Chris. "They Keep Calling Me: The Crow's Transference of Trauma into Art." *Film Obsessive*, October 23, 2019. https://filmobsessive.com/film/film-features/film25yl/they-keep-calling-me-the-crows-transference-of-trauma-into-art/.

Flashback FilmMaking. "Behind the Scenes «The Crow» (1994)." YouTube, January 27, 2017. https://www.youtube.com/watch?v=hmaimTyH56g.

*Fort Worth Star-Telegram*. "Brandon Lee Follows Father's Footsteps." *The Baltimore Sun*, August 25, 1992. https://www.baltimoresun.com/1992/08/25/brandon-lee-follows-fathers-footsteps/.

Fox, David J. "'The Crow' Takes Off at Box Office : Movies: The Opening Is the Biggest Ever for Miramax. In Second Place Is 'When a Man Loves a Woman,' with 'Crooklyn' Third." *Los Angeles Times*, March 6, 2019. https://www.latimes.com/archives/la-xpm-1994-05-16-ca-58401-story.html.

Gonzalez, Umberto. "'The Crow': Everything We Know About the Reimagining So Far." *The Wrap*, March 15, 2024. https://www.thewrap.com/the-crow-remake-everything-we-know/.

Grambush, Jacklyn. "A Brief History of Grunge: The Seattle Sound." Culture Trip, April 9, 2019. https://theculturetrip.com/north-america/usa/washington/articles/a-brief-history-of-grunge-the-seattle-sound.

Weiss, Arlene R. "Interview with 'The Crow' Author, Artist, Musician James O'Barr: 'Let the Picture Tell the Story.'" *Guitar International*. October 4, 2011. Archived November 14, 2011. https://web.archive.org/web/20111114095911/http:/guitarinternational.com/2011/10/04/interview-with-the-crow-author-artist-musician-james-obarr-let-the-picture-tell-the-story/.

Wigington, Patti. "The Magic of Crows and Ravens in Mythology." Learn Religions, July 19, 2024. https://www.learnreligions.com/the-magic-of-crows-and-ravens-2562511.

Wikipedia. "Brandon Lee." April 10, 2003. https://en.wikipedia.org/wiki/Brandon_Lee#Death.

Wikipedia. "Method Acting." July 28, 2024. https://en.wikipedia.org/wiki/Method_acting.

## Acknowledgments

This is my first book and a dream come true. My biggest and most loving thanks go to Jen Sookfong Lee, who often understood my ideas and put them to words better than I ever could. A dreamy writer and kind editor, Jen has shaped this book into a celebration of a film that deserves more impassioned consideration than it has received. I feel I have grown so much with her guidance and careful eyes and immense patience with all my ideas and words! Thank you for believing in me; this book is yours as much as it is mine. A further thanks to ECW Press for having me; I feel so immeasurably proud and grateful to be in the company of such glittering giants. Thank you to Carrie Gleason and Victoria Cozza for your editing genius.

I would also like to thank all of the editors who have worked with me up until now and offered me advice; each one has shaped me in big and small ways, and I am eternally grateful for the trust they put in me. Most of all, though, I would like to thank Carl Broughton and Katie Duggan at *Film Daze*. Katie nurtured my curiosity and allowed me such a beautiful, roaming space to explore ideas as a baby film critic — she challenged me to be confident as I teased out ideological links between everything from Susan Sontag and *One Hour Photo* to our medical traditions and *Ginger Snaps*. But most of all, she allowed me the freedom to write this book's predecessor, "The Weight of Feeling: How 'The Crow' and 'John Wick' Embody Kurt Cobain's Grunge," which is excerpted throughout the latter half of this book. *Film Daze* has saved me so many times over the course of the past few years — thank you, Carl and Katie. I wouldn't be here without you.

Finally, I would like to thank myself. Not in a weird, vain way, I promise! I am proud of myself for this book. I am proud of myself for sticking around. And I am proud of myself for my curiosity, for continuing to read even when it was tough, for building the little library that has become an invaluable point of reference; writing this book, I often would turn behind me and pluck out a book from my shelves that I bought years before, as if intuiting that I would need it now. I love writing about movies and thinking about them with respect. I hope I get to do this for the rest of my life.

**Alisha Mughal** is a culture writer based in Toronto. She is a journalist and film critic who has written for *Film Daze*, *Exclaim!*, RogerEbert.com, and *Catapult*. She was born in Pakistan and studied philosophy at the University of Toronto and journalism at Humber College. *It Can't Rain All the Time* is her first book.

**Entertainment. Writing. Culture.**

ECW is a proudly independent, Canadian-owned book publisher. We know great writing can improve people's lives, and we're passionate about sharing original, exciting, and insightful writing across genres.

**Thanks for reading along!**

We want our books not just to sustain our imaginations, but to help construct a healthier, more just world, and so we've become a certified B Corporation, meaning we meet a high standard of social and environmental responsibility — and we're going to keep aiming higher. We believe books can drive change, but the way we make them can too.

Being a B Corp means that the act of publishing this book should be a force for good — for the planet, for our communities, and for the people that worked to make this book. For example, everyone who worked on this book was paid at least a living wage. You can learn more at the Ontario Living Wage Network.

This book is also available as a Global Certified Accessible™ (GCA) ebook. ECW Press's ebooks are screen reader friendly and are built to meet the needs of those who are unable to read standard print due to blindness, low vision, dyslexia, or a physical disability.

The interior of this book is printed on Sustana EnviroBook™, which is made from 100% recycled fibres and processed chlorine-free.

ECW's office is situated on land that was the traditional territory of many nations, including the Wendat, the Anishinaabeg, Haudenosaunee, Chippewa, Métis, and current treaty holders the Mississaugas of the Credit. In the 1880s, the land was developed as part of a growing community around St. Matthew's Anglican and other churches. Starting in the 1950s, our neighbourhood was transformed by immigrants fleeing the Vietnam War and Chinese Canadians dispossessed by the building of Nathan Phillips Square and the subsequent rise in real estate value in other Chinatowns. We are grateful to those who cared for the land before us and are proud to be working amidst this mix of cultures.

**ecwpress.com**